RUGBY PARTNERSHIP

RUGBY PARTNERSHIP

John Rutherford and Roy Laidlaw
with Norman Mair

STANLEY PAUL

LONDON · SYDNEY · AUCKLAND · JOHANNESBURG

TO OUR FAMILIES
AND FRIENDS

Stanley Paul & Co. Ltd
An imprint of Century Hutchinson Ltd
62-65 Chandos Place, London WC2N 4NW

Century Hutchinson Australia (Pty) Ltd
20 Alfred Street, Milson's Point, Sydney 2061

Century Hutchinson New Zealand Limited
PO Box 40-086, Glenfield, Auckland 10

Century Hutchinson South Africa (Pty) Ltd
PO Box 337, Bergvlei 2012, South Africa

First published 1988
Reprinted 1988, 1989
Reissued in paperback 1989

© John Rutherford and Roy Laidlaw 1988

Filmset by SX Composing Ltd, Rayleigh, Essex
Printed and bound in Great Britain by Scotprint Ltd, Musselburgh

British Library Cataloguing in Publication Data
Rutherford, John
    Rugby Partnership.
    1. Rugby Union football. Player – Biographies
    I. Title II. Laidlaw, Roy
    796.33'3'0922

ISBN 0 09 174147 5

Contents

'The telepathic understanding of Roy Laidlaw and John Rutherford was such that it was always said that they could find each other in the dark, and for Roy it was never quite the same with any other stand-off. In Dublin Airport, on the morning after Scotland's defeat at Lansdowne Road in 1988, Roy, in search of the loo, came upon a gaggle of somewhat bedraggled Scottish supporters. One of them looked up. "Still looking for Richard Cramb?" he enquired, sympathetically.' – NORMAN MAIR in *The Scotsman*

Acknowledgements

John Rutherford and Roy Laidlaw would like to thank Norman Mair for all his help in writing their book. Thanks also to Colorsport, *The Scotsman, Glasgow Herald, Daily Express, Daily Record, Southern Reporter*, David Stranock, Bob Thomas, *Cork Examiner* and Mike Brett for the use of their copyright photographs.

*Roy being presented to The Princess Royal, Patron of the Scottish Rugby
Union, by the Scotland captain, Colin Deans*

Foreword

As Patron of the Scottish Rugby Union, I am happy to write this foreword to *Rugby Partnership*. With my own involvement in international sport I know something about what is needed to perform at the higher levels. To remain at the top of your sport for a decade, as John Rutherford and Roy Laidlaw have, one needs the desire born of a genuine love of the sport and a notable measure of consistency in terms of performance. Rutherford's widely acknowledged tactical awareness and Laidlaw's tenacity and courage were saluted throughout the game – two contrasting styles combining to produce a formidable 'rugby partnership'.

With both hailing from the Scottish Borders, steeped in the traditions of rugby, it was natural for John and Roy to become great friends. With a world record 35 appearances together in major internationals, and so many matches together, it is no wonder they feel they have experiences to share and opinions to offer. Leading participants in any sport have a worthwhile contribution to make to the next generation of sports people and – with the help of Norman Mair's knowledgeable, perceptive and entertaining writing in collaboration with Scotland's record-breaking half backs – many past, present and potential players, as well as spectators, will gain enormously from this book.

HRH THE PRINCESS ROYAL

Jim Telfer

Prelude

On the evening of Sunday 24 April, 1988, in the Albany Hotel, Glasgow, the Variety Club of Great Britain (Scottish Committee) gave a dinner to John Rutherford and Roy Laidlaw. The sporting personalities present ranged from Ireland's Willie John McBride, manager of the 1983 Lions to New Zealand, to Terry Butcher, of Rangers and England. Something in the region of £12,000 was raised towards the cost of sunshine coaches albeit not, as the Reverend Howard Haslett mischievously suggested, for the benefit in their twilight years of the two old gentlemen in whose honour the company had gathered but on behalf of the handicapped. The evening was entertainingly compered by Dougie Donnelly, of BBC Scotland, and there was much scintillating oratory by a cast which included the afore-mentioned Rev Howard Haslett; John Dawes, captain of the victorious 1971 Lions; Allan Hosie, the former international referee; Brian Meek, Scotland's Columnist of the Year; and Willie John McBride. The main speech of the evening, though, had been reserved for Jim Telfer, coach to Scotland's 1984 Grand Slam side and a man constitutionally incapable of any tribute he did not mean.

The greater part of the text of an address which earned Telfer a standing ovation is given below.

Mr Chairman, Honoured Guests, Gentlemen, if you are involved in active sport, there are some occasions which are special. Some occasions you never forget.

The occasion may be some great victory or event where you feel great pleasure and pride in being part of that event or that victory.

When you grow older, when you have a sedentary, more detached role, you treasure such occasions with even more relish. Gentlemen, I believe that tonight we have just such an event – this occasion when all of us are here to honour John and Roy for their contribution to rugby football.

Laidlaw's Corner. Roy diving through the despairing tackle of Willie Duggan to score in the 1984 Triple Crown match

To be asked to come to such a dinner is an honour, to be asked to speak, to be quite honest, frightening. It was made even worse a few weeks ago when I met Walter Thompson who writes for the Sunday Post under the guise of Fly Half. We were talking about John and Roy and when he realised that I was speaking at a dinner given by the Variety Club of Great Britain, he said, 'Oh, you'll have to make it funny. . .' If I had been frightened to speak before I was now even more terrified.

When I sat down to write a few notes, I found it difficult – not to find words about John and Roy but to decide what to miss out. Quite honestly, I could write reams about all the players I have coached over the years but obviously John and Roy come into that category with a vengeance.

When you consider that I first watched John as a 17-year-old playing for the Scottish Schools in 1972 and that since then I have known him in the relationship of coach and player, and that I actually coached Roy for the first time when he was playing for the South of Scotland Under 21 XV in the early 1970s, well, you can see my problem.

Great players to be so classified must be able to do great things on the rugby field and, to do great things on the rugby field, you must possess great skills. As rugby players, Roy and John, in my opinion, are dissimilar in many ways. Each has his own brand of attributes – each is his own man.

There is a uniqueness about each of them. I am convinced that in years to come, whether it be in Jed or Selkirk, or in other parts of the Borders and Scotland, youngsters will strive to copy them – to be a stand-off like John or a scrum half like Roy. In that sense they may be copied but there is very little possibility of their ever being emulated.

When I think of Roy, if I may take Roy first, I think of a coiled spring, full of potential energy, ready to let rip. I think of a real battler, always taking the game to the enemy, courageous, prepared to give his all every time he goes on to the field, be it for Jed or the South, for Scotland or the British Lions. Sometimes, indeed, to the point of recklessness. Sincerely, Gentlemen, pound for pound, Roy is the bravest player I've coached.

He has taken batterings off the field as well as on it. Although he was for so many years a top class scrum half, I think I am right in saying that he was twenty-six before he was awarded his first cap and the fact that he then went on to play international rugby for nine years speaks volumes.

A player who had to work constantly on his service and on his kicking to keep them at the appropriate level, Roy is a naturally aggressive, combative type of player with or without the ball. Two of his greatest strengths are his tackling and his break.

Quick off the mark, he is a superb cover tackler and just yesterday, in the Jed sevens, his tackling all over the field was the talk of the tournament. He was also a great fringe tackler of big forwards coming through the lineout or on the edge of loose play.

Yet, above all, he was a tremendous breaker, the best I have ever seen, especially in how consistently he brought it off. That's praise indeed, Gentlemen, when you remember that, over the years, I have seen Sid Going, Terry Holmes, Jerome Gallion and Gareth Edwards, to name but a few.

Imagine, Gentlemen, a scrum right of centre field, thirty yards out and offering an oblique, big blind side, channel one ball, quick delivery. Roy taking off for the try-line like a greyhound out of a trap. . . .

Whether it be against the Ireland B in 1979, when he scored two tries, or versus Waikato for the 1983 Lions when he scored a magnificent try in the same fashion, or yet again in the Irish matches of '84 or '86, that will be my lasting memory of Roy Laidlaw. Sprinting with the ball in two hands, going for the line, attacking the defence and, invaluably, letting his support come in behind him.

John Rutherford oozes class. Beautifully built for a stand-off: good balance, strong hips, a natural runner whose style had to be changed to suit the pressure of the game at the top. Not a natural kicker, John worked and worked on improving this aspect of his game until he became a prodigious line-kicker and also an excellent tactical kicker, be the kick in question the high up-and-under, the grubber, the diagonal or a drop-kick.

I was fortunate that in every Scottish team I coached except one, against Romania in 1981, John and Roy were the halfbacks. Almost always I could rely on them for a top-notch

John Rutherford, British Lion

14

performance both individually and as a unit.

John thinks about the game a great deal and I spent many hours talking rugby with him. Although a quiet bloke, he is fiercely competitive. He wants to win every time and this rough edge rubs off on other players in the side.

It may have been that under me his running style was a little curbed but I hope that he will never blame me for this, while feeling that his other strengths were encouraged. Quite frankly, Gentlemen, for me, when I coached the Scottish side, he ran the show. He controlled the game and if he played well, we played well.

We all know about the innumerable games on TV around the world in which John and Roy have featured. We've watched some great matches but the best I ever saw Scotland play, while I was the coach, was not in the British Isles or even all that much in the limelight but on our tour of New Zealand in 1981. That afternoon Scotland beat Canterbury and just to give you a measure of how good they were, let me say that Canterbury were the Provincial team whom many a touring team feared most.

They had beaten Lions' teams all too consistently but Scotland that day defeated them 23-12. To me, as I say, that was the best performance which Scotland ever achieved with me and, of course, John and Roy were at the heart of it. The one pity of that victory was that it took place twelve thousand miles from home and few, other than the touring party and two or three Scottish rugby writers, were there to savour it.

As with Roy, I have many outstanding memories of John. I recall when he was chosen as inside centre for the Lions in the Third Test in 1983 and he was played there simply because he was the best footballer we had around. He scored a lovely try but, unfortunately, was injured and did not play in the Fourth Test.

I remember 1981 and level pegging against Australia at Murrayfield, time nearly up. Ball from the lineout, a high kick from John to the posts, Roger Gould, the full back, slightly out of position, misses it. It bounces and there is Jim Renwick to pounce and score under the posts, a Scotland win. . . .

Although his kicking became legendary, it is as a runner that my abiding memory of John will be. Ireland 1984, the second half and Roy departed with what they call 'athlete's migraine'. To the ordinary player it may look very like concussion but one very big difference is that with concussion you are not supposed to play again for three weeks!

Scotland won a ball from the lineout on the left-hand side and Gordon Hunter, on as the replacement, broke across the pitch and fed to John. In his own inimitable way, he jinked inside the defence and drew the inside centre before feeding back out to Keith Robertson who scored at the posts. Wonderful stuff.

Against England the same year, the second try of the match. A twenty-two drop-out to England, the kick to the Scottish forwards who work it back to Roy. His chip over the top is gathered by Dusty Hare but the ball is smuggled off him by Jim Calder. A Scotland drive precedes a tremendous ruck and a copybook layback to Roy.

John picks the pass off his toes, jinks inside but slips the ball on out to Euan Kennedy who scores by the posts. Those two pieces of brilliance will always be with me when the conversation turns to John Rutherford.

But not just those two incidents. So much of what I see in the mind's eye of John, my vision of him, will be as the runner he was by nature. Picture any match with John at stand-off. We've just scored a try and the opposition kick-off. It could be for Selkirk, for the South or for Scotland. The ball kicked deep into our twenty-two. John fields, dummies to kick to touch but instead steps off his right foot and takes off, ball in two hands, running left. The counter-attack is on. John as I shall remember him.

Many other players have heard me say this countless times before. Rugby is an individual sport first and a team sport second. John and Roy have been great individual players but their real contribution has been as a combined unit.

They have been partners in thirty-five major internationals, eighty-four major representative games while, of the eight internationals they missed as a pair since they first appeared together in 1980, let me just say that Scotland lost seven. Remarkable statistics.

Over the years, I have spent many hours with Roy and John,

Roy in Jed-Forest colours

on a rugby field, in hotels, travelling abroad. Both have been excellent ambassadors for rugby and for Scotland, on and off the field. Roy with his pawky sense of humour, John with his boyish pranks.

Seasons ago, when I was in charge of the B team, John and Roy were in the side and I was speaking to the young players who, as always at that level, were very excited and ambitious. I said that I hoped they all did well and went on to play for Scotland but I added, 'Never forget where you come from. Never forget that you are the lucky ones among the thousands who have failed to make it. Always remember to be modest, to be humble and always be loyal to your beginnings.'

Gentlemen, after forty-two caps and forty-seven respectively, after Lions' tours, after Scottish tours, after a World Cup, after being at the top of international rugby for a decade, John and Roy remain modest, unassuming young men, un-affected by fame.

Above all, they remain fiercely loyal to their first loves, their clubs, Selkirk and Jed, to whom they have given unstinted service over the last fifteen to twenty years. They have been a shining example of what can be achieved from humble beginnings and I trust that their example will spur more young men from their towns to do the same.

John and Roy – thank you for your unique contribution to rugby at so many different levels. It has been my pleasure to know you, to work with you. We've savoured the ecstasy, we've suffered the agony and it has been a great privilege for me to speak about you tonight.

John and Roy – I salute you.

Roy Laidlaw

1 The Border Cradle

The occasion marked the first game together for John Rutherford and Roy Laidlaw. The Selkirk stand-off displayed some fine touches and must benefit from a game at this level. Rutherford and Laidlaw look the part and a lot more will be heard of this pair – Scottish Border Club Under-21 *v.* Champagnat of Argentina Under-21 at Melrose, 1974 – *Southern Reporter.*

My first rugby ball fell off a lorry.

Before the fuzz closes in demanding rather more detail, I should perhaps add hurriedly that it was my grandmother, Peggy Laidlaw, who found it on the road and dutifully took it to the police station. It was never claimed and, if the unwitting donor happens to chance upon these paragraphs, perhaps it will be some compensation for his loss that no rugby ball was ever more proudly prized.

My grandfather, John Scott Laidlaw, had played for Langholm and my grandmother had seen Scotland defeat England at the opening of Murrayfield in 1925 to win their first Grand Slam. She is still an ardent follower of the game and attends all Jed-Forest's home matches at Riverside Park. She is a great lady and a great character whom the cartoonist, Giles, might have found a rich source of inspiration.

On the day of her eighty-fifth birthday, we were playing West of Scotland at Riverside, the family party to celebrate the occasion being scheduled for the evening. Ten minutes from the end I got a bang in the face, which left me badly swollen in the vicinity of the eyes and nose and with blurred vision, the damage causing me to leave the field.

I was sitting in the changing-room feeling sorry for myself when the rest of the lads trooped in at no-side. Not far behind was a minor commotion caused by my grandmother who was bent on seeing me and assessing the injury. Some of the lads had already stripped off and, though her glasses had steamed up from the bath water, that maybe made it all the more alarming as she pushed across the room less by sight than by braille. She cast one dismissive glance at what was a darned painful injury and declared, firmly, 'That's not much, you'll be at the party tonight!'

Neither of my parents was of rugby stock but my father, Ian, took such an interest in the semi-junior club, Jed Thistle, that he was elected to the committee. My mother, Ina, was terrified of the game and only once in all my career plucked up enough courage to come and see me play. The match was against Langholm which was scarcely calculated to reassure her. In the event, I was briefly poleaxed by a high tackle which prompted her to retire to the car.

John's father, Bill Rutherford, was from the West and he and his wife, Helen, were initially much more interested in soccer, Bill being on the committee of Selkirk FC in the East of Scotland league for whom Helen made the teas. But, very much as happened in our clan, once his sons were playing for the Selkirk Youth Club, Bill switched allegiance and, until his death three years ago, was on the committee of the Selkirk Rugby Club, and it is for them that Helen now helps out on the catering front.

Helen braved the spectating pressures and perils rather longer than did my mother but, for most of John's international career, she and her twin sister, Mary, would watch on television with a bottle of brandy handy in case of crisis. John's two complimentary tickets went to his father and the uncle after whom he was named, John Young, who had fetched Helen by car to the hospital on the night Scotland's most capped stand-off was born.

I had my first real taste of rugby at Jedburgh Primary. It was love at first sight, perhaps not least because the coach, Rod Sharp, did his stuff so well. He taught us the basic skills with an emphasis on tackling for which I perhaps owed him a great deal in later life. He would set up situations with four players coming at you and you had to be able to tackle off either shoulder with your head in the right place and a proper drive into

(left to right): Bruce Craigie, Robert Hall, Robert Laidlaw. Middle row: Robert Thomson (committee), Alan MacDonald, George Aitchison, Robert Lindores, Tam Elder (committee), Andrew Minto, John Mercer, Norman Richardson, Jack Kirkpatrick (committee). Front row: Charles Haig, Roy Laidlaw, John Laidlaw, Derek Hill, George (Papa) Forbes (coach), Alec Fairbairn (committee), Bruce Hickman (captain), John Coppard, Kenneth Lyall, Lorance Bunyan

impact. No sooner had you made one tackle than you had to get up and make the next.

Of course, like most small boys, we preferred to play rather than go through some of the sterner practice chores but the two years I had in the Primary XV were invaluable. Nowadays mini-rugby at Riverside Park on a Sunday morning is so popular with the small boys that the minister at the church, on the principle that, 'If the hill will not come to Mahomet, Mahomet will go to the hill', has moved one of his Sunday schools to the rugby ground!

21

John was at Philiphaugh Primary next door to the Selkirk ground and, by the age of nine, he was in their seven as a hooker. Sevens played the major role there as elsewhere in the Borders. Aside from matches against the rather older boys in the first year of Selkirk High School, the Philiphaugh Primary geared their rugby towards the two great highlights of their season, namely, the Border Primary Schools sevens tournament and their own separate encounter with the rival primary in Selkirk, Knowepark.

Each primary put three sevens in the field, the ties being played in the one afternoon at Philiphaugh with the entire town turning out to watch and the wee fellows having to cope with the whole pitch. The odds were on a final between the A sevens from the respective primary schools which, of course, provided the ideal climax.

While at Philiphaugh Primary, John was coached by John Torrie, an erstwhile threequarter who had played in the Selkirk side shortly before the unofficial Scottish club championship was won and who wasted scant time in translating John from a hooker into a stand-off. John has never been slow to acknowledge his debt to Torrie. He still recalls how such moves as they had were named Ettrick, Tweed and Yarrow after the local rivers, and how Torrie taught him the dummy and that, if he looked away to the apparent recipient, the tackler's own eyes would follow. Yet, of all the things Torrie taught John, one of the simplest is the one for which he is most grateful: that, as an inside back, he should never get into the habit of tucking the ball under one arm but always carry it in two hands ready to show it to friend and foe, pass it or kick it.

In John's day, Philiphaugh Primary won the Border Primary School sevens at Netherdale and one of John's most treasured cuttings contains a comment from Bill McLaren, the justly famed BBC television commentator, who has also done a marvellous job for Hawick rugby as an itinerant physical education teacher at primary level. McLaren, in saluting the achievement, confessed that he had never even heard of Philiphaugh Primary before they emerged as winners against an entry which included such Hawick primary strongholds as Burnfoot and Drumlanrig.

Philiphaugh Primary School, winners of the Border Schools Sevens Cup. John is in the centre

After primary school, I moved on to Jedburgh Grammar where the physical education master in charge was Bill Johnstone, nephew of Bill McLaren and nowadays himself BBC Scotland's chief radio rugby commentator. He had been a reserve for the South Under-15 XV in their annual match with Wales and, though a little lightly built for a senior forward, had played for Jed-Forest at senior level. He was enthusiastic and continued our rugby education along the right lines. He also took country dancing which I hated but which was the only alternative when the weather caused rugby to be cancelled. We would be on one side of the room and the girls on the other and Bill would call, 'Take your partners.' Inevitably, the prettier girls were the ones mainly in demand and John always swears that that was the origin of my acceleration over the first ten yards.

I left school at fifteen, the more academically inclined in those days going on to Hawick High School. I had made enough of a mark in the Jedburgh Grammar School XV to be chosen for a trial for the South Under-15 XV but a broken wrist kept me out of that game.

At Selkirk High School, to which he had gravitated from Philiphaugh Primary, John played all the indoor sports such as volleyball and basketball and at one point was playing rugby for the school on a Saturday morning and for the Selkirk Youth Club in the afternoon before turning out at soccer for the British Legion boys' team on the Sunday morning. He took it all in his stride but thinks now that it was probably too much and tends to agree with Leslie Allan, the former Melrose and Scotland threequarter, who argues that there is a case for school matches being played in mid-week in the Borders, leaving the boys free to turn out for the clubs' age-group teams on the Saturday.

Partly because of his father's background in football, John, something of a Rangers fanatic to this day, was at one time keener on soccer than he was on rugby but that soon changed as he began to make his way in the latter code. At Selkirk High School, where he was eventually Head Boy, he was in the First Year team which beat Hawick High School at that level for the first time in history. The talent he had shown at primary school was soon growing still more evident.

Both John and I were probably lucky in that we were the middle of three brothers which meant that we were never short of someone with whom to play, the Rutherford fraternity playing shooting in from the street against the door of their garden shed where the Laidlaws, with less of a soccer backcloth, were probably devising one against one rugby games.

My older brother, John, played for a couple of seasons on the wing for Jed-Forest and later for Corstorphine while my younger brother, David, was a scrum half cum utility back who had perhaps more natural ability than either of us but was somewhat slightly made. When he can get away on a Saturday, he still turns out for one of Jed's lower XVs.

John's elder brother, James, revealed quite a lot of pace in his years on the wing for the Selkirk Youth side and later knew what it was to wear the Selkirk jersey at First XV level. His younger brother, Billy, played seven or eight seasons for Selkirk as a wing or a centre and more recently has thrown in his lot with Peebles. He was in that winning Philiphaugh Primary seven with John and, in the years that lay ahead, they were to feature together in Selkirk sevens which won their own tournament, and at Kelso.

Billy, as John will tell you, rather enjoyed a bit of needle and there was a memorable afternoon in a sevens tie at Netherdale when Peter Dods was away down the touchline and Billy came across and tackled him. Billy, in pushing himself up, stuck his hand in Peter's face and an incensed Peter took a swing at him. In the ensuing exchanges, the Gala touch-judge was moved to join in, smacking Billy across the head with the touch-flag, the referee, Allan Hosie of the International panel, being too convulsed with laughter to intervene.

One of the great strengths of Border rugby, in the opinion of both myself and John, is the structure of semi-junior and junior rugby. I first played for Jed Thistle at fifteen while John was in the Selkirk Youth side at fourteen, facts of life at which many in the cities would no doubt throw up their hands in horror. Players did not leave the semi-junior scene until they were nineteen and that meant that there could be a huge disparity in ages – especially as some of the matches which, say, the Selkirk Youth Club played were against grown men in senior clubs' Third XVs.

On paper, one would probably have to agree that that kind of thing is very dangerous but, frankly, neither of us believes that it did us any harm. Rather the reverse. A great deal clearly depends on the individual, particularly in the matter of upbringing and background, physique and temperament.

In our day, the three leading semi-junior teams were the Selkirk Youth Club, Jed Thistle and Hawick PSA, and both John and I knew the heady glory of winning the Border semi-junior league. In the town of Selkirk a boy like John was always keen to support the school by playing for them but there was no doubt that the Selkirk Youth Club were *the* team in the eyes of aspiring youngsters. They were coached by the former Scotland hooker, Jock King, who was assisted by Glyn Smith who had been a back. John recalls that they played a very basic game with much importance attached to winning secure first phase possession; a good deal of kicking in support of the forwards and territorially; and some mostly orthodox back play.

Jock was quite a legend in the town and had a great influence on the up and coming players. It was a great tragedy that he died relatively young.

At Jed Thistle the coach was the old Jed-Forest forward, George Forbes, more generally known as Papa Forbes. He was everything to us and, not being married, would join us for our long Sunday walks, the conversation invariably never far away from rugby. He was an ardent advocate of sevens and there was something of the sevens style in the way that Jed Thistle played.

John always contends that one of the greatest sevens ties he ever saw was the clash of Jed Thistle with Melrose Colts in the final of the Jed Thistle sevens. It was a thrilling engagement in which the winning try was scored for Melrose by none other than Andy Irvine who, as all the world knows, subsequently reverted to Goldenacre and Heriot's F P.

Papa Forbes – who, very touchingly, presented me with his well worn tracksuit not all that long before he died – had not had as distinguished a playing career as Jock King but, in his own manner, he was no less an institution in Border semi-junior rugby circles. Not only was he a compelling coach for teenagers at that stage in their rugby lives but he was something of a father figure, albeit one with his own inimitable ways. Once, in a match with Langholm opposition, I came by an accidental but deep gash in my leg and, worried about it, sought out Papa Forbes who by then was with his cronies in the committee room. Papa inspected the wound and then, dipping his forefinger into his whisky, rubbed the alcohol into the gaping cut, 'There,' he said, 'that will do you' – and it did.

John stayed at Selkirk High School until he was seventeen, collecting five highers and gaining entrance to Jordanhill College of Physical Education. He played once for the Scottish Schools, versus England at Netherdale, the victorious Sassenachs having Alastair Hignell at scrum half and John Scott at lock. John was a little in awe of the boys from the city schools and, though he did not like to say so, was totally bemused by his scrum half who informed him that he always fed his stand-off at sixty degrees. Nevertheless, it was a profitable experience partly in that it gave him a taste of the international environment but more specifically because the coach was Jim Shearer from Galashiels Academy, who taught John much with regard to positioning, angles and the like.

At seventeen, I left Jed Thistle and joined Jed-Forest, receiving an unexpectedly early baptism when I was taken as a replacement to the Ardrossan sevens and was quickly on the field as one of the Jed players was injured.

I made my debut for Jed-Forest not as a scrum half but as a centre in a match with Edinburgh University in which I scored a try. It was by then a straightforward club fixture, whereas in bygone years the legendary Colonel C. M. Usher used to bring down his own university XV to play Jed-Forest in a game outside the unofficial Scottish Club championship, but which gave rise to one of the best Riverside stories. Playing for the students, Gus Black, the Scotland and British Lions' scrum half, who generated such an extraordinary length of pass that the Edinburgh University medical authorities were said to have taken a plaster cast of his wrists, was breaking through when he was unceremoniously tripped, going head over heels: 'Keep your bloody feet down, Black,' roared a Riverside regular.

I was never dropped by Jed-Forest until last season when, after I had shared in a defeat of Hawick, the club preferred Gary Armstrong. I won my place back but I have the greatest regard for Gary. I would name him, along with Derek Hill, who was in the same primary school team as I was, George Turnbull, who often partnered him in the centre, and Robbie Lindores, on the flank, as outstanding Jed-Forest men of my time. Gary is tough and competitive and, as he showed in his debut for the Scotland B against their Italian counterparts, has a good break and an eye for the line. He has, though, the same shortcomings in terms of his service as haunted me for so much of my career, in that he is not yet at all good off his left hand. The difference is that, well coached though I was in so many ways, I never had anyone in my earlier years to din into me the importance of correct footwork if the ball was to be swept away without that often disastrous preliminary backswing; and of practising passing maybe ten times as much off the weaker hand as off the stronger, at any rate until a proper balance had been achieved. Gary has it in him to be a tremendous player for Jed-Forest, the South and Scotland, while in the queue just behind him at Riverside is another very promising scrum half in Grant Farquharson. He is nothing like as well endowed physically as Gary and so I have endeavoured to stress with him that he will have to make up for that not just by appropriate weight training and so forth but by quickness and skill resulting from hard and intelligent practice.

They should be spared the sudden shock of realising, as I did on my elevation to senior and representative levels, that where you can probably break almost at will in school and semi-junior rugby, an inadequate service is now going to be shown up as never before. I had soon appreciated the importance in senior rugby of strength, stamina and speed, and had been prepared to spend part of the close season working alongside professional sprinters. But I never cease to kick myself for not having got down to the classic rudiments of a good service sooner, though it amazes me that there was not more available to me in the way of the right kind of instruction in that particular aspect of the scrum half's portfolio. To be fair, I was not alone in suffering in this way and I should like to think that my service, even at its worst, never deteriorated to the standard of one otherwise redoubtable England scrum half who was once dismissed immortally by Steve Smith as, 'The one with the Barnes Wallis pass' – a wonderful image of the ball bouncing along to the be-leaguered stand-off.

John made his debut for Selkirk in the Gala sevens and, in the very first tie, scored three tries against Glasgow Academicals. Not so long ago, in a pub in Ireland, a seeming stranger came across the room and exclaimed, 'You don't remember me?' John didn't but it was his opposite number in the Glasgow Academicals' seven from that day and, hardly surprisingly, he had most certainly not forgotten John.

A bad car crash rudely interrupted John's career. He and his brother, Billy, were returning home from a holiday in Wales in the car they had borrowed from their brother, James, when, just after they had passed through Langholm, they hit a lorry. The police adjudged that John, who was driving, must have fallen asleep but they took no proceedings. Billy was concussed and sustained cuts but not only was John cut about the face from going through the windscreen but the steering wheel had

The South Under-21 XV – John and Roy's first match as a partnership. Back row (left to right): Robbie Lindores, Billy Turnbull, Ian Easson, Bob Cunningham, Gordon Dickson. Middle row: Jimmy Johnston, Les Allan, George Miller, Roy Veitch, Andrew Ker, Gordon Smith, Brian Hislop, Billy Murray, Robin Charters, Jim Grieve, J. Barnfather, Billy Patterson (trainer). Front row: Nick Guise, John Rutherford, Roy Laidlaw (captain), Bruce White, George Telfer, George Fairbairn

broken some ribs, one of which pierced a lung. Yet, oddly enough, it was the apparently lesser injury to an ankle which kept him out of rugby for a season and postponed his arrival at Jordanhill by a year.

They were frustrating months for John for rugby was now the main interest in his life as it was in mine. Indeed, I can remember how on Fridays, when studying at Galashiels College of Further Education for my City and Guilds qualifications as an electrician, my mind would always stray to the next day's rugby.

John had been in the cricket XI at Selkirk High School but, unlike his brother, Billy, did not play for the Selkirk senior XI, though Selkirk had a considerable tradition in cricket as well as in rugby. Actually, though we did not get cricket at Jedburgh

A youthful Ronnie Cowan – a great inspiration to John

Grammar School, many Border rugby players turn naturally to cricket in the summer months and it was when being driven at the speed of light by the Burrell brothers from Gala to a Test match at Headingley, that the then aged Selkirk cricketer, Jock Grieve, made his oft-quoted retort.

'At this rate,' said one Burrell brother to the other with satisfaction, 'we should be there in time to watch some of today's play.'

'At this rate,' said Grieve, whose heart had been in his mouth for many a mile, ' we could catch some of yesterday's as well!'

When John did go to Jordanhill, Bill Dickinson, still the driving force of Jordanhill rugby, was naturally keen for him to play for the club but John, as one would have expected, remained loyal to Selkirk just as he was to do when he was a master at George Watson's College and therefore eligible to play for Watsonians. He did turn out for the College in mid-week matches and in the British Inter-College tournament in which they twice in his day reached the final but by now, of course, he was very much a focal figure in the Selkirk XV.

Apart from any other factor, he would not have wanted to have let down David Bell, a lock forward not far short of the higher representative class who was to become a decided personality at Philiphaugh first as captain and then as coach. His alliance and friendship with Bell was a key element in John's burgeoning rugby career but another to whom he owed much was Ronnie Cowan. As an eighteen-year-old, Cowan had gone with Scotland to South Africa in 1960 and had returned to that country with the 1962 British Lions before going on to make a name for himself in Rugby League.

Cowan invited Jock Turner, the Gala, Scotland and Lions' midfield back, to have a look at Rutherford and then passed on Turner's very perceptive comments. Sometimes Cowan would turn up in his Rugby League Leeds Cup Final jersey and there came a time when he received a letter from the S R U warning him off. John continued to go to Cowan's house to talk rugby, while he still looks back fondly to those numerous occasions when Cowan would come down to Philiphaugh early to kick with him or would bring along a couple of junior players so that he could put John through his paces in given situations.

31

Roy Laidlaw for Jed – a great try, a great photo

It goes almost without saying that John, like so many Borderers, has never seen why Rugby League players should be treated like lepers and, what is more, often by the same people who can't wait to insinuate themselves into the company of such other professional sportsmen as a Jack Nicklaus, a Nigel Mansell or a Virginia Wade. Patently, Rugby Union has to have some safeguards to protect itself but neither John nor I can quite see how turning to Rugby League, which is not even the same game, can make a bloke like Alan Tait, who signed at the end of last season for Widnes, a good guy one day and a villainous outcast the next.

It is really only the Borders which have been the target for Rugby League scouts though, heaven knows, Andy Irvine had his share of lucrative offers. Jed-Forest have suffered more than most in losing major personalities who would otherwise have put much back into the club and it is perhaps just as well that not all the scouts know their business.

In Wales one of them, who was after a player the club assuredly did not want to lose, was told conspiratorially in the local pub that there was, in fact, another who was an even better prospect. He fell for it, signed him at an exorbitant fee without watching him play and then lived to see the day when the directors of the Rugby League club concerned hauled the player in and told him he was to be transferred.

'For what?' enquired the player, sensing a share of the transfer fee.

'For ever!'

Both John and I count ourselves thrice blessed that we were reared in the Border rugby cradle, though you do not have to journey far afield to be reminded that even those who are household names in the Border country are apt to be of small account elsewhere. By illustration, I should just cite the eve of an international in Edinburgh when the team went to that charming cinema, the Dominion. The manager was gracious enough to have the lights turned up and to ask the audience to welcome the Scotland team. It was a very nice gesture and the standing ovation we received was greatly gratifying to our egos until, as the applause died away, an awed voice was to be heard calling reverentially, 'Which one is Kenny Dalglish?'

2 Peaks, troughs and the Grand Slam

Of the Scots no one had made a greater contribution than John Rutherford. His judgement was perfect, he couldn't be faulted in any way. Roy Laidlaw's support was crucial too, and, when either one kicked, they chose the right club and hit the green – DICK GREENWOOD, England coach, in *The Year of the Thistle.*

At half back Laidlaw and Rutherford were magnificent. If Laidlaw was the inspiration with his two brilliant tries, Rutherford was the steady influence throughout – RICHARD SHARP on Ireland *v.* Scotland 1984 in the *Sunday Telegraph.*

Laidlaw was a real thorn in our side. I believed we had devised tactics to contain him but when the match got going there was simply no way he was to be stopped – WILLIE JOHN MCBRIDE, Ireland coach, in *The Year of the Thistle.*

I would never claim to be all that well versed in English literature but John and I got to know Kipling's two imposters, Triumph and Disaster, on either side of the Grand Slam and, indeed, around the heady glory of that coveted feat.

Thinking back over our representative careers, I find myself dwelling first on the blunt reminder of different standards at representative and international level which we received from the All Blacks at Mansfield Park in 1979. We were in what we thought a very good and confident South XV, and when I run over the names I can see why. P. W. Dods; K. W. Robertson, J. M. Renwick, A. G. Cranston (captain) and D. J. Ledingham; J. Y. Rutherford and R. J. Laidlaw; J. Aitken, C. T. Deans, N. E. K. Pender, A. J. Tomes, T. J. Smith, J. M. Berthinussen, G. Dickson and C. B. Hegarty.

Thirteen of that team are in the roll of Scottish internationals and yet we were trounced 19-3. Our coach was Derrick Grant, whose views on the All Blacks and appreciation of their virtues were not dissimilar to those of Jim Telfer. He had sought to impress on us how good they were, that we owed it to ourselves to play out of our skins because, in a sense, it was a privilege to be on the same field.

You could argue that it was a dangerous line to take because, if he overdid it, we would be liable to take the field overawed but, if there were two opinions on that, there was only one on whether his assessment of what we faced was right or wrong. The All Blacks, set against their own remarkable history, had had a poor tour of Britain in the early 1970s while many of the side at Mansfield Park that afternoon had still to become the household names they later were. Players such as Graham Mourie, Murray Mexted, Dave Loveridge and Stu Wilson meant very little to us when we tripped on to the field but, within moments of the kick-off, we got a rude insight into what Derrick Grant had meant when he talked about pressure.

The All Blacks' kick-off was deflected down to me which was not quite according to plan and I passed quickly to John who got his kick away in a twinkling. But Mourie had blazed straight on past me and actually got his fingers to John's punt. It found touch but John knew then what was to come. We were badly deflated by the result and it was obviously a sad disappointment to Grant who was destined to be Scotland's coach in the World Cup quarter-final at Lancaster Park in 1987. Grant Wilson, the Scotland Under-21 prop, owes his Christian name to the fact that his father was a great admirer of the rugby played by the three Grant brothers – Jake, Oliver and Derrick – but it was pure coincidence, much though he admired Derrick, that John called his second son Grant. Not that that stopped us from calling him, tongue-in-cheek, 'a crawling *****!'

Still more humbling was the rout of the South by the All Blacks at Netherdale in October 1983 by which time the coach was Johnny Gray of Gala, who was to have a memorable run in the Inter-District championship. Jim Aitken, who was down to captain the side, had to withdraw with Keith Sudlow, my Jed-Forest clubmate, being the late replacement. Nevertheless, it was no bad side the All Blacks decimated: P. W. Dods;

A. M. Thomson, G. R. T. Baird, K. W. Robertson and I. Tukalo; J. Y. Rutherford and R. J. Laidlaw; K. Sudlow, C. T. Deans, R. F. Cunningham, A. J. Tomes, T. J. Smith, D. B. White, I. A. M. Paxton and D. G. Leslie. The South had murdered Wellington at Netherdale not all that long before, but New Zealand on tour were another proposition. The blend at lock of the two big men, Alan Tomes and Tom Smith, did not work out and our tackling, particularly in terms of the first tackle which knocks opponents back before they can get started around the fringes of scrum, ruck and lineout, disintegrated. So bad was it that Jim Telfer, in a typical touch, made us watch the video of the later stages of the match on the Friday before the Triple Crown game with Ireland in 1984. He did not say anything, just left us to sit there wincing at our inadequacies.

At international level, there have also been matches which went sorely wrong. None hurt more than the drubbing we took from New Zealand in the Second Test of our 1981 tour, the score that afternoon at Eden Park being 40-15 with a try-score of 7-1. We had played some very good stuff in the First Test at Carisbrook Park in Dunedin in losing 11-4 with a try-score of 2-1 and many thought we might have won. The All Blacks came in for some stick in the press afterwards from which we caught the backlash in Auckland. The real tragedy of that Second Test was that, as Stu Wilson and Bernie Fraser conceded in their very readable book, *Ebony and Ivory*, we played far from poorly for much of the match.

With the game still in the balance, Jim Calder had what we thought was a good try disallowed and then, with the All Blacks leading 22-15, Steve Munro, possibly the fastest man on the pitch, intercepted deep in his own half but with room to spare. Had he scored it would almost certainly have been under the posts and at 22-21 – assuming Andy Irvine had kicked the simple conversion – anything might have happened. As it was, Bernie Fraser got across to take Munro who, to be fair, had not been too fit before the match and was running through the heaviest part of the field. The real lesson of that match, and one which was not wasted on Jim Telfer who did not make the same mistake in Australia in 1982, was that we trained too hard, too long, too close to the game.

In retrospect, it is easy to see that we had worked so hard during that tour that there was no way we were going to fail at Eden Park on the score of fitness. We could therefore have taken the week much more lightly while still honing our drills and skills. Jim Telfer would be the first to admit that he always had to guard against a tendency for his own enthusiasm and insatiable appetite for rugby to run away with him.

The preparation of Scotland teams in our time became so good that it would be unfair to be too critical, but that same error recurred more than once under other coaches. It was revealing to hear Jim Craig, of Celtic and the Lisbon Lions, saying on the radio how amazed he always was to hear that Scotland had had a strenuous three-hour session as late as the Thursday before a match. But, of course, in defence of the coaches, they are not dealing with full-time professionals and so often have the feeling that there is still a lot to do. In contrast, before the World Cup match with France in Christchurch, Scotland eased off their preparation from the Tuesday onwards very much as professional soccer teams would have done.

The 1988 Calcutta Cup was a disastrous match and not just because we lost but because it was such a shocking advertisement for rugby with so much that was purely negative and destructive. The most regrettable feature of all was that as outstanding a coach as Derrick Grant should end up being accused of whingeing, because one of the traits of the man was that he had always taken defeat very well in public, no matter how hard it hit him. It was simply that the player and the coach in him were outraged, and if England saw the game differently from us, that is hardly anything new in international sport. It was a game apart and not one locked in the memory alongside those previously mentioned defeats at the hands of the All Blacks or such failures as the Second Test in Australia in 1982 or that painful match with England at Twickenham in 1987.

One of the ironies of that 1987 England engagement was that we had two of the best training sessions John and I can remember on the Thursday and Friday before the match, but maybe that just went to prove the wisdom of that adage about a good and bad rehearsal.

We were mobile but light in our front five with no great

lineout presence. The better rugby brains in Scotland, among the press and the SRU hierarchy, not to mention elsewhere, had worried that a team who took us on up front, whose forwards drove with their backs kicking in support so that we had scant chance to get the ball back once we had lost it, would expose our limitations. England, with their mountainous pack, did just that and did it well, but we played miserably and tactically contributed to our own defeat.

It was a wet day but, instead of changing our tactics as we had done on the morning of the 1984 Calcutta Cup at Murrayfield, we played too much of the match with what little ball we had as if it were a dry day. Moreover, in the absence of Scott Hastings, our midfield of John, Keith Robertson and Roger Baird, for all their rugby ability, were collectively very light. Even as it was, England scored their two tries only because we gave the ball away, though there was no denying that they had much the better of the game and deserved the win which denied Scotland a second post-war Triple Crown.

As to that heavy reverse in the Second Test in Australia, it came at the end of what had been a notable year for Scotland. In Cardiff, we had thrashed Wales by five tries to one in winning 34-18, their first defeat within the International Championship on their own ground since France won 14-9 in 1968. It was also Scotland's first win in the Welsh capital since 1962.

Before that Welsh match we stayed not in the city centre but out at the St Pierre Golf and Country Club with the backs having a last training spin on the golf course on the morning of the game. Jim Telfer painted the picture of us in the guise of the SAS, in and out of Cardiff on a swift but lethal strike. In the event, that was very much as it turned out and yet, for the first twenty minutes, John and I both thought we could be on a hiding. Then came Jim Calder's try from a break-out brilliantly instigated by Roger Baird and, for all that much of our own attacking originated in Welsh mistakes, we could scarcely do anything wrong thereafter.

Jim Renwick, in simultaneously winning his forty-seventh cap and enjoying his first away win in a Scotland jersey, had the game of his life. John dropped a lovely goal, the best strike, he thinks, among the twelve he dropped for Scotland. The try he

38

engineered with David Johnston for that quick-footed fellow to rip through the Welsh defence was still being played over and over again the next day by such a connoisseur as the late Carwyn James.

In 1988 fourteen of the Welsh players left the post-match dinner in Cardiff before the speeches. On the evening of that historic Scottish victory in 1982, Gareth Davies, the Welsh captain, got to his feet and, in lieu of the conventional speech, merely asked his players and the assembled company to join in the singing of the 'Flower of Scotland' as a tribute to Wales's conquerors. A gracious gesture.

One other memory from that year in Cardiff was of Telfer, before the match, dinning into us how lucky we were and how much we owed to those who gave great but much less glamorous service to the game. At the right moment he brought in John Law, the long-serving SRU secretary, who stood there looking sheepishly appreciative as Telfer extolled his contribution.

Scotland had no great record Down Under having lost the waterlogged Test with New Zealand in 1975 24-0 with a try-score of 4-0; and, aside from that hefty defeat in the Second Test in Auckland in 1981, having lost to Australia in 1970 at Sydney 23-3 with a try-score of 6-0. None the less, we had really begun to believe in ourselves. Since the 1981 tour to New Zealand, which was itself the beneficiary of the short tour in 1980 to France with Jim Telfer as coach, we had returned home to beat Romania, Australia, Wales and France and, though we lost to Ireland, draw with England.

The Australian tour did not begin too auspiciously but we learned quickly from the matches with Queensland and Sydney and then gave a tremendous display in defeating New South Wales 31-7. We had found the Australian deployment and tactics behind the scrum setting us new problems with their three inside backs lying very close together and quite flat. They looked sitting targets for offensive-defence but they moved the ball so swiftly with quick, short passes that the sudden long pass would throw us. Their back three, comprising the disengaged blind-side wing, the full back and the open-side wing, were devastating in the way they would come on to the ball at pace and different angles.

We were scrummaging so well that we were able to change our defence with Jim Calder, at flanker, taking the stand-off or first five-eighth and the rest of the backs drifting out one. It proved a resounding success and, after the New South Wales match, their captain, Michael Hawker, congratulated us on having done our homework so shrewdly and thoroughly. The other big factor in our first Test match win Down Under, the 12-7 defeat of the Wallabies at Brisbane, was that a new Australian coach had taken over in Bob Dwyer, and he had gone for a running game with Mark Ella at stand-off and Glen Ella at full back rather than a kicking stand-off in Paul McLean and a big strong full back in Roger Gould.

We actually celebrated when we heard the Australian XV because, for all the talents of the Ella brothers, we considered we had them worked out. In the Test itself, they were booed by the Brisbane crowd, who bitterly resented the omission of the Queensland players, McLean and Gould.

The Australians changed their team and their tactics for the Second Test in Sydney bringing in McLean and Gould and, though we were already trailing, it did not help our cause that it began to rain after twenty minutes. We were well beaten 33-9 with a try-score of 3-0, but it was still something to have drawn the Test series 1-1. The win in the First Test gave us our second away win of the year after the barren seasons in which Scotland had not won away since that terrible match with Ireland in 1976, a game which Scotland won by four penalty goals and a dropped goal to two penalty goals and in which, when the enfabled Mike Gibson left the field before the end, a scribe asked him if he were 'actually injured or only bored!'

In 1984 Andy Slack's Grand Slam Wallabies, under the inventive coaching of Alan Jones, slaughtered Scotland 37-12 at Murrayfield, scoring four tries with a wet ball without reply. But that day, as was once said of the Wallabies' compatriot, Sir Donald Bradman, 'poetry and murder' lived in them together and, besides, Scotland's Grand Slam team had begun to break up. Neither John nor David Leslie played that afternoon, Scotland's 'Great White Shark', John Jeffrey, playing the first match of his colourful Scotland career and Douglas Wyllie also

40

making his debut in place of John. Still more significant, Jim Telfer, whose men the Grand Slam squad were, was no longer the coach.

There were many factors behind the winning of the Grand Slam in 1984. The advent of the national leagues in 1973-74, the acceptance of coaching at senior and representative level and innumerable squad sessions all played their part. Another factor was that those who can go back a lot further than either John or I rate that 'Big Five' the best S R U selection committee in living memory, all former players of district level and four of them Scottish internationals. Bob Munro, who was to manage Scotland in the World Cup and who is now the convener of selectors, was the one uncapped, the others being Ian MacGregor, the convener, Robin Charters, Jim Telfer and Colin Telfer.

Yet, in the last analysis, nothing mattered more in the build-up to 1984 than the overseas tours beginning with the 1977 Far East venture under Nairn MacEwan as coach which blooded such as myself, John, Colin Deans and Keith Robertson. Then came those much more exacting trips to France, New Zealand and Australia. Nor was it just the Grand Slam players who benefited. The Australian tour, for example, gave invaluable experience to Finlay Calder who, having been on the point of retiring from the representative scene when Jim Telfer suggested to him that he could have an international future if he shifted to open-side wing forward, is now one of the great players on the international stage with a ball-playing dexterity rivalling the legerdemain of the Tricolors.

Those tours taught us so much, not least when it was sheer folly to rush headlong in offensive-defence in the midfield, the Wallabies and the French often liking nothing better. Again, in 1981 under Jim Telfer, an All Black at heart, the Scotland rucking went from strength to strength, the forwards taking the second phase 27-5 against Wairarapa Bush, whose coach was none other than Brian Lochore. A grand No. 8 and captain of the 1967 All Blacks of fond memory, Lochore was the overall coach in charge when New Zealand won the World Cup.

On that 1981 tour Scotland beat Canterbury 23-12 and, which was entirely relevant to what was to come, Jim Aitken captained the team that day in the absence of Andy Irvine. The forwards were the first-choice Grand Slam eight of three seasons later and the half-backs John and myself. In other words, the front ten were those of 1984.

There was, too, another facet in that the Lions in New Zealand in 1983 had no fewer than eight Scotland players in the party – myself, John and Roger Baird behind the scrum, and, among the forwards, Colin Deans, Iain Milne, John Beattie, Iain Paxton and Jim Calder. John, for one, says that he went out there with perhaps a touch of an inferiority complex as regards the players from the other countries but came home feeling that he was at least as good as most of them, if not better. We learned also a lot about the individual strengths and weaknesses among the opposition we would face in the International Championship and Jim Telfer no doubt learned even more.

Very importantly, the South players who had been butchered by the All Blacks at Netherdale got their confidence back under Jim Telfer when they drew 25-25 at Murrayfield, the second draw in a series dating back to 1905 in which Scotland have still to record their first win. But then Wales have never beaten South Africa, while Scotland, despite that 44-0 massacre at the hands of the Springboks in 1951, have defeated them thrice.

The equalising try was scored from a rehearsed diagonal by David Johnston, a ploy which went much better in the match itself than it had in practice. The scorer of the try, which Peter Dods could not convert, was Jim Pollock, 'Lucky Jim' who came in for Keith Robertson at the eleventh hour for the Welsh match of 1982 and who was never on a losing side until his seventh match for Scotland, against Romania in Bucharest in 1984.

In the weeks between the game with the All Blacks and the match in Cardiff with Wales, the Scots were brought back to earth with myself, Iain Paxton and David Leslie among those who played for the Whites or junior team in the national trial. The Whites then proceeded to win 21-3.

By now, under Jim Telfer as coach and Ian MacGregor as convener of selectors, Scotland's build-up to an international was well nigh perfect and we were too good for a Wales XV in

Jim Calder snatches the try which turned the Grand Slam match with France

Cardiff who were going through the transitional process. As so often when you have won, we could look back and see where we had had the breaks, notably in the excellent move which brought Iain Paxton's try which certainly contained one pass which looked suspiciously forward. But then, as they say in soccer, you don't get awarded doubtful penalties if you are never in the penalty box and we were the better side. In that we were helped by the extraordinary Welsh decision to play Richard Moriarty not only on the flank but off the tail of the lineout where he had no chance of matching David Leslie's voracious winning of the ball on the ground and where he was so out of his element that he was even outclassed by Leslie in the jump.

England came to Murrayfield having not played for a month, though how much of a disadvantage that is remains a matter for argument. The match was won on the Saturday morning when Jim Telfer returned to the hotel after his habitual personal inspection of ground conditions and the prospective weather and changed our tactics which had been to run the ball rather more than previously.

The game plan now was to get the ball down on the deck

43

whenever possible and to turn the heavier-footed England forwards by hoisting the wet ball up into the wind and by long, skidding diagonals. John had noticed from studying England on video how far up their wings, John Carleton and Mike Slemen, lay and he rightly deduced that there would be any amount of room behind them. His tormenting of Dusty Hare that afternoon compounded the sorrows of that great servant of Leicester who had so unhappy a day with his goal kicking that his wife, for the first time since they were married, could bear to watch no longer and slipped quietly from the ground.

The Scotland rucking that day was at its zenith, particularly in the prelude to the try in which John plucked up my pass adroitly, wet ball or no, and did just enough to allow Euan Kennedy to thrust exultantly over the England line. On the debit side, Scotland lost in the course of the match Bill Cuthbertson, whom Telfer deemed just about the best rucking forward we had – though, mind you, he had nearly lost him much sooner. On the Australian tour in 1982, on the Great Barrier Reef, Gulliver, as we called him, got caught in the rip, that deadly tide or current feared even by accomplished swimmers, let alone by someone like the Scotland lock who, though he had told nobody, could hardly swim at all. At first the players ignored his cries, thinking he was fooling – and it was almost too late when they suddenly realised he was not and Alan Tomes and Jim Calder plunged to the rescue. Cuthbertson was compelled to wear for the rest of the tour a T-shirt emblazoned Jacques Cousteau.

I often ponder what might have happened in 1984 if Hare had kicked his goals, just as the record 33-6 defeat of England at Murrayfield in 1986, when our back five in the pack of assorted No. 8s ran them off their feet, would surely have been a very different game had Rob Andrew had a better day with his goal kicking. Nor would the game have followed the same pattern, even if it had produced the same result, with a dry ball – the mere thought of a wet ball always bringing back a story which Jim Renwick swears is true. Namely, of a match at Langholm when Hawick were greatly looking forward to having a dry ball to handle and Renwick, on his way to the pavilion loo, came upon the match balls swimming in the bath!

The Irish match was won and lost in the first quarter and Willie Duggan's decision to play against the wind, though it had been the practice of the great Welsh teams of the early 1970s and of many other modern teams besides, brought all manner of criticism down upon his head. Ireland had played England at Twickenham and the message of that match, as so often against those green jerseys, was that the one thing we must not do was tee up our midfield backs for the Irish to smash into them and create splintered ball behind our gain-line. Obviously, we would have to drive up front and endeavour to get in behind them either by attacking through the back row and halves or by suitably inquisitive punting.

It went like a dream with Alister Campbell, who had taken over from Cuthbertson as front jumper and lineout sweeper, doing much to set up one of my two tries by driving round the lineout to set up the juiciest of rucks. It was Scotland's first Triple Crown since Wilson Shaw's match of 1938 and it culminated fittingly in a beautiful try in which Roger Baird unselfishly sent in Peter Dods in the corner.

I had had to leave the field with a head knock to be replaced by Gordon Hunter, who did very well and had a large hand in the try Keith Robertson scored from another masterly piece of rugby by John. At one point, I was in doubt for the French match towards which our expectations of success were hardening by the day.

At first, after Lansdowne Road, there was simply the relief that we had at last won something but, having got the taste of success, we wanted that Grand Slam. France had by far the better of the first half and they believe to this day that the Welsh referee, Winston Jones, the third referee in our four matches who was making his international debut, let us away with all kind of transgressions but most pertinently off side when we were pressurizing them. I do not say that they did not more than once, in the matter of off side particularly, have cause for grievance but we felt that we suffered no less from his reluctance to allow rucks to develop which robbed us of one of our main weapons.

In the end, we won going away from them with Jim Calder's opportunist try from a lineout on their line also leaving them questioning the referee. Yet I shall always agree with those who aver that the Grand Slam was really won by the fanatical defence of the first half in which we not only did our best to compromise their possession from scrum, ruck and lineout but tackled with the utmost tenacity and the new belief we had in ourselves.

No-one would normally have been more loath to pick out an individual from such a great team performance than Jim Telfer, but he could not forbear to nominate Iain Milne as our Man of the Match. His scrummaging was immense and he took enough punishment to have put many a heavyweight boxer on the floor, yet still came back for more.

In its own way, the 20-20 draw with France in our first match in the World Cup on the neutral soil of Lancaster Park, Christchurch, was no less meritorious, especially in view of the loss of Scott Hastings before the match and John so soon after the start. Nor was there any disgrace in going down to the All Blacks in the quarter-final on the same field. We were fairly and squarely beaten but, further beset by injuries as the team by then were, the players gave their all and the try-score of 2-0 not only compared more than favourably with the 8-1 roasting Wales received in the semi-final but with the 3-1 by which France succumbed in the final itself.

One of the regrets which John and I share is that neither Jim Renwick nor Andy Irvine shared in the Grand Slam, though Irvine, on the bench on the day of the French match, got as close as being told to warm up as cover for not one but two players who had taken a knock. The roar he would have received from the crowd had he come on would have been worth hearing and the French reaction interesting. They have never forgotten what Andy Irvine, in addition to other exploits in other years, did to them in 1980. After making all sorts of errors and missing several kicks to the point where he was actually being got at by the crowd, he turned a 14-4 deficit around with two astonishing tries to end a long losing sequence by Scotland.

The Grand Slam, Scotland's first for fifty-nine years, will come to mean more, not less, to us in the years to come even though we fervently hope that the wait this time will be dramatically shorter. It is said in Scotland that you can tell a rugby

John Carleton and a triumphant John Rutherford leave the Murrayfield pitch after the 100th Calcutta Cup

man now simply by word association. Say 1984 to most folk and they will reply, 'George Orwell': say 1984 to a member of the rugby fraternity and the answer will be, I wager, 'Grand Slam'.

Grand Slam Players (excluding ourselves)

For Jim Aitken, see Chapter 5; for Iain Milne, see Chapter 3; for Colin Deans and David Leslie, see Chapters 3 and 5.

Peter Dods (Gala). Peter Dods was not physically imposing and, indeed, even had a touch of the knock-kneed about him, but he was a revelation in the Grand Slam team as the man called upon to fill the boots of so vivid a personality as Andy Irvine. He was a safe fielder and generally a reliable line-kicker without being terribly long. He was no sledgehammer when it came to tackling, not least because he was not that strongly-built, but he was plucky and had some very good tackles to his name. Not a counter-attacker in the Irvine mould, he was very good at turning up outside the open-side wing. However, it was as an accurate goalkicker that he really made his mark in the Grand Slam season, passing Irvine's 1979-80 record haul of 35 points for Scotland in a Championship season. His 50 points contained just the one try against Ireland. Quiet and unassuming, he was an admirable tourist who would never complain.

Steve Munro (Ayr). Just under six feet but endowed with a strapping physique, Steve Munro was quick and quite elusive but his main asset was his strength. Very powerful in the thigh and leg, he could break tackles and was often used for a crash ball through the middle of a defence. In the auxiliary full back duties expected of the modern wing threequarter, he was not in the same class as, say, Roger Baird but he did improve considerably over the course of his career. He was a sound hard tackler.

Roger Baird (Kelso). Relatively lightly-built in an era turning more and more towards threequarters with the build of flank forwards, Roger Baird tackled more than his weight and was partly responsible for the badly needed improvement in Scotland's blind-side defence down their own left flank. An accomplished and versatile footballer, he was a wing who later played for Scotland as a centre, which was frequently his berth for Kelso for whom he also played stand-off. He played scrum half for Scottish Schools and Merchiston Castle, though it was on the wing for Kelso that he won his first Melrose winners' medal while still a schoolboy. He scored a try for the British Lions in the Third Test in 1983 in New Zealand and was a prolific try-scorer for the South, but he found that coveted first try for Scotland frustratingly elusive. Nevertheless, his own unselfishness had contributed to that blank scoresheet while, partly through his gift for counter-attacking, he made some unforgettable tries for others – most memorably detonating the moves which ended with Jim Calder's try against Wales in 1982 and the try by Scott Hastings versus England at Murrayfield in 1986. Usually cheerful and always friendly, he contributed much to the team spirit which was one of Scotland's greatest strengths in 1984.

Jim Pollock (Gosforth). 'Lucky Jim' was a very useful footballer but perhaps an even better mascot for it was not until the seventh of his eight matches for his country that he was on a losing side. Although capped by Scotland on the wing, Pollock played much of his club rugby at stand-off, which no doubt had something to do with the huge punt he had developed. In fact, he was more a utility player than a great specialist in any one berth. He was not particularly quick as international wings go but there were cleverer angles to his running than might have been apparent to the untutored eye. On his debut against Wales at Cardiff in 1982 he got one of Scotland's five tries and, still more famously, scored the last-minute try when Scotland drew 25-25 with the All Blacks at Murrayfield. He was great company, his Geordie accent giving its own dimension to many of the squad's favourite Scottish songs.

Euan Kennedy (Watsonians). No doubt about it, Euan Kennedy will be remembered first and foremost as a devastating tackler, the head-on tackle being his speciality. At the higher levels, he had to contend with a certain lack of real pace but, well built at 6ft 5in, very tall for a centre, he knew how to make the most of his strength and was used by Scotland to set up rucks in the middle of the pitch. It was as a full back that he had gone with Scotland to Japan in 1977 and his ability to punt was a useful feature of his play at inside centre. A beautiful passer, he could change the area of attack with one long spin pass. He was one of three brothers, the Kennedy family being almost as much a part of Myreside as the stand and clubhouse.

David Johnston (Watsonians). Probably the quickest man in the side over 15 metres, David Johnston had searing acceleration. At his best, he could exploit a genuine outside break and he was a tireless worker both in support play and in defence. As befits a former Hearts footballer, he could use his feet brilliantly with the ball on the ground but strangely he was not a great kicker and did not drop goals. His passing and distribution were not his strong suits, but he was a tigerishly courageous tackler who appreciated how valuable speed off the mark like his was in pressurizing opposition defences, be it in pursuit of a kick or to get in a follow-up tackle. Although David gave the impression of being somewhat laid back, he was an intelligent and conscientious trainer who got himself very fit.

Keith Robertson (Melrose). One of the most complete players yet given to inconsistency, Keith Robertson had great skills and could be, on his day, world-class. A lovely, ethereal player to watch, he could swerve, sidestep, kick, and pass stylishly both ways. He could on some afternoons be too much of an individualist from the point of view of those outside him, which was partly why Scotland tended to play him on the wing where, additionally, his ability under a high ball was often in evidence. A light-footed runner without anything remarkable in the way of sustained and finishing speed, he himself preferred centre where, against England at Twickenham in 1985, he scored a try in which his balance as he ripped the defence apart defied the laws of gravity. He had a resilient attitude summed up in his often reiterated creed of 'take the rough with the smooth' and was a great companion.

Gordon Hunter (Selkirk). A very strong scrum half who revelled in the physical side of rugby, Gordon Hunter, when my understudy, had the advantage of being John's regular club partner. Endless practice at squad sessions is all very well but, for instance, matches together under fire in the Border League constitute a much better grounding for a man suddenly ejected from the substitutes' bench into the international maelstrom. A good kicker and a forthright tackler, Gordon Hunter had worked on improving his service, often with his wife Nancy acting as a stand-off. Presumably she was suitably grateful that he wasn't a prop. More than once in his career he came back after an injury which would have finished a lesser man, and it was typical of his luck that he should fracture his cheekbone in a collision with a spectator as he ran exuberantly from the pitch after sharing in the Triple Crown win at Lansdowne Road.

Alan Tomes (Hawick). Probably better appreciated by his fellow players and opponents, both at club and representative level, than by some pundits, though it would be fair to say that just as he could rise to the occasion so he could be very ordinary when not motivated. Among the big men of his time in Scotland, and there were not very many, he was the one with the hardness, the one who knew when not to stand politely on ceremony. Reared in the Hawick school, he had been well taught, one curiosity of his career being that Scotland mainly jumped him in the middle of the lineout whereas he had always had a hankering for the role of front jumper. His pressing ambition to play in the World Cup prolonged his career, but even by the year of the Grand Slam his penchant for cropping up in the open had already brought him three tries from lock forward, not to mention those for which he had provided an 'assist'. Dubbed by his team-mates the world's greatest tourist – he toured every year from 1975 through to 1987 – he is an entertaining raconteur and was as important a character as he was a player in the Grand Slam squad.

Bill Cuthbertson (Harlequins). By the yardstick of the 1980s, Bill Cuthbertson, at 6ft 3in, was a little lacking in height to be a great lineout exponent, and, to be honest, his best work at that set-piece was done in the realms of sweeping and, as his appearance suggested, the more piratical aspects of ball-winning. A solid scrummager, Cuthbertson, a tough hombre, was a real player's player and a rucker who satisfied even so demanding a connoisseur as Jim Telfer. Known as 'Gulliver' because of his aversion to travelling (rather as the tennis player Rod Laver acquired the nickname of 'Rocket' when a small boy because that was precisely what he wasn't), Cuthbertson was no bad vocalist and consequently found himself lumbered with the organisation of the squad's singalongs.

Alister Campbell (Hawick). Campbell came into the Scottish team in 1984 for the Irish match as the replacement for the injured Bill Cuthbertson. A very different man and in some ways a dissimilar player, he nevertheless had some of the same virtues not least as a lineout sweeper. A little bigger than Cuthbertson, he had rather more potential as a lineout jumper, but especially in his baptismal year he was not quite as crafty or streetwise, but then neither was he as liable suddenly to give away a blatant penalty. Another schooled in the Hawick tradition, Campbell was the genuine article as a Border forward, a real grafter who yet had his more spectacular moments, particularly on the peel round the lineout. A comparatively unobtrusive member of the squad but a solid trooper.

Jim Calder (Stewart's Melville F P). Ubiquitously mobile rather than fast, Jim Calder was a superbly perceptive support player with an ability, when tackled, to make the ball available not excelled by any forward in the world. To him goes a major share of the credit for the huge and crucial improvement in Scotland's blind-side defence at scrums to the left of the Scottish posts, and on occasion he was prepared to trust the forwards to maintain the initial shove and himself break early to police his port-side station. Against Wales in Cardiff in 1984, he rather overdid it, getting too wide and no longer giving his man only one way to go but, a very intelligent player receptive to good advice, he was never likely to make the same mistake again. Not really quick enough to play as an open-side flanker off the tail of the lineout, he was eventually somewhat overtaken by the shift in thinking towards having four big men in the pack. However, he was a good tidier-up as third man from the end and, as France found to their cost in that 1984 summit meeting at Murrayfield, a quick-witted ball-playing opportunist. As a player he lived and had his being perilously close to the offside line but, away from rugby, he always struck both of us as a straight-up-the-middle citizen. Definitely the quieter half of the Calder twins.

Iain Paxton (Selkirk). An outstanding athlete – not too many forwards have scored a solo try from under their own posts as he did against Wales in 1985 – Iain Paxton had a good build and the ball-sense of a former Scottish Schools basketball international. A middle-of-the-line jumper on occasions for Selkirk, he was much more profitably placed towards the tail of the lineout in the international arena, winning some very usable possession for Scotland in the latter station. John, who saw so much of him in a Selkirk jersey, always rated him brilliant at kick-offs, whether rising to catch or deflect one from the opposition or sweeping up to attack the recipients of a kick-off or drop-out from his own side. He had that almost indefinable something we call class and his great rival, John Beattie, who was in a better position to know than most, reckoned him a much harder and more uncompromising forward than was widely supposed. He was subsequently to play for Scotland at lock, and play pretty well, but his optimum berth was No. 8 and it was there that he was chosen for all four Tests on the British Lions' tour of New Zealand in 1983.

John Beattie (Glasgow Academicals). An explosive and abrasive forward, Beattie looked the authentic article from the day he played his first B International, taking all sorts of flak from the French as he went up for the ball at the lineout but looking as much at home in those exchanges as if he played every week in their first division rugby. As one wag said, you would have

Members of the Grand Slam team 'off to meet the Queen'. From left to right: Val and Johnny Gray, Ruth and Jim Aitken, Hazel and Peter Dods, Joy and Roy Laidlaw, John and Alison Rutherford, Keith and Alison Robertson, Colin and Val Deans, Jim and Francis Telfer

thought he had his own café in the south of France. An aggressive runner, ball in hand, which is how he came by the injury against England in 1987 which ended his career, he was an uninviting player to tackle. A lineout jumper who very definitely believed in the old biblical adage that it was more blessed to give than to receive, he was exceptionally good in the reduced lineouts which Scotland, when short of towering height at lock, were forced to employ. He lost a little bit of speed after suffering the first of his serious knee injuries before the Scotland 1981 tour of New Zealand but he was still anything but slow. At No. 8 he exhibited the necessary control of the ball at his feet and I always found his distribution on the pick-up to my liking. Away from rugby, John Beattie played in a rock band and on tour would borrow a guitar and let rip.

Each of the following was one of the six nominated replacements for one match or more: Andy Irvine (Heriot's F P), Douglas Wyllie (Stewart's Melville F P), Stuart Johnston (Watsonians), Rob Cunningham (Bath), Gary Callander (Kelso), Norrie Rowan (Boroughmuir).

3 Great Players
David Leslie – my best and meanest

Roy Laidlaw's enthusiasm thus far into the season is astonishing. His skilful tracking and trapping of opponents who were very much fleeter of foot demonstrated his immaculate judgement of time and distance – CHRIS REA *on the Gala Centenary sevens in* The Scotsman.

In New Zealand John Rutherford bit so deep into even the All Blacks' defence that Murray Mexted was used from No. 8 in the Second Test in close collaboration with the relevant flanker and the stand-off to blanket the threat he posed. Moreover, so the informed word was, at least one other forward was specifically detailed to be on the look-out for Rutherford slicing back inside – NORMAN MAIR *in the* Sunday Standard, June 1981.

By the time John and I broke through to international rugby, Andy Irvine was already established as by far the greatest box-office attraction in Scottish rugby. John believes to this day that he was the best player against whom or with whom he ever played, not in the sense of being the most complete but because he could touch heights, have passages of brilliance, beyond the reach of others.

His fielding during his career was far from flawless. Apparently, in his earlier years, he was prone to take the catch front on and far below the level of his eyes which all too often were not on the ball anyway but on his next move. He learned to make the appropriate half turn under a high ball, and the cradle of hands and arms, and when in that text-book position he made very few mistakes. He was, as he was the first to concede, no J. P. R. Williams as a tackler but he was much better than some of his detractors allowed and over the years got in some good and vital ones. It was not his strong suit but he was very competitive and had the ability and reactions to adjust his sights quickly and retrieve seemingly lost situations. He had both pace and acceleration and his ability to stop or check and then go was one of the things which made him so dangerous. John tells of a one against one practice the two of them evolved and of being considerably disconcerted to find how often and easily Irvine beat him and how unexpectedly difficult he was to get past.

Andy would beat a man not with the chattering side step of the Welsh but with a jink which was all his own, partly side step and partly swerve. He had far more strength on his feet than many might have imagined to go with his thirst for the enemy line. John swears that he never saw another player who so often contrived to get up in bursting support after having been tackled and that, of course, argues a very high level of physical fitness. John and I always believed that, in the manner of New Zealanders, he must have done a great deal of training on his own to supplement team sessions. He was quite often to be seen running over the golf course of the Merchants Golf Club which was near where he used to live.

The 600 metre runs which we did in training can be a killer but Andy held the record. He always knew how important to him was that fine edge to his speed and, once it began to go, he was the first to acknowledge that he was not quite the same player. John who, as a stand-off, was in an ideal position to judge, admired his vision which was reflected both in his reading of play and in his running off the ball.

Andy always saw himself as somewhat akin to a striker in football. In fact, not only was he a gifted opportunist and finisher but, in common with the like of Jimmy Greaves, he was to be judged on what he could do rather than the things he couldn't or didn't do. As John avers, neither of us ever came across a player who could so captivate his admirers. Out in New Zealand, despite the difficult games he so often had against the stifling and remorseless pressure of the All Blacks, he had a huge following.

To me, David Leslie was at once the best and meanest player I ever encountered. I do not mean by that that he was a dirty player who would gouge eyes or land a premeditated kick on

David Leslie, who lived and died by the law of the Kamikaze but who also knew how to use the ball

the head of a player on the ground but, psyched up for the big occasion, he lived and died by the law of the Kamikaze. He always let the opposition know that he was there and he was no more loath to tread on a player on the deck than an All Black. A fifty-fifty ball was almost always his, and it was in going for one that his forearm smashed into Jerome Gallion in the Grand Slam match with France in 1984. The French scrum half was stretchered from the pitch amid momentary alarm that he was not going to come to.

David was not all that much over six foot in height, and well-built rather than heavily so. Yet John used to say that when he was playing stand-off against a David Leslie acting as the enemy tail-gunner, he was always taken aback by how big he suddenly seemed. Yet, lethally physical though he could be, what really turned him into something special was that he was also so skilful. He had played stand-off as a young boy at Glenalmond and you could see it in his ability to take and give a pass, to field and kick. His ball-sense was no less valuable when it came to securing the ball on the ground, in which area of rugby he was almost in a class of his own. His dexterity, added to his timing, compensated for any lack of inches at the tail of the lineout where he was frequently nothing less than brilliant, notably against France in 1983 and in the Welsh match of 1984.

Personally, though Scotland needed him as an open-side flanker and he did extremely well in that role, I always thought his optimum berth was No. 8. When Jed-Forest played against Gala and he was at No. 8, his use of the ball was always exemplary and it was difficult not to envy his scrum half.

It was a mystery to his contemporaries why he was left out of the 1983 Lions' tour to New Zealand, though the word was that important voices in authority thought that good though he was, he did not play wide enough. No one, though, must have been more surprised by his omission than Graham Mourie who used to be all over the field himself and who, after watching David Leslie have a game of games against the Tricolors in Paris in the months before the Lions' tour, put him down at once as an absolute banker. The Lions' selectors, mind you, watched that match only on television and that may have cost Leslie dear.

He was always regarded as a rather reluctant trainer but, on a Lions' tour, he would have got very fit. Moreover, he was in his element against the All Blacks. He used to give as good as he got, and sometimes more, against them. John has vivid memories of sharing a room with him on the night before the Second Test on Scotland's tour of New Zealand in 1981. He heard a kind of grunting and moaning coming from Leslie's bed and, when he turned on the light to see what was wrong, Leslie was lathered in sweat, already living the next day's match. Remembering how many All Blacks he had attempted to dent, or caught with a boot when rucking, he was in no doubt as to what he could expect to receive in return on the morrow but, of course, as usual was all set to take the battle to the foe.

Jim Renwick was another great Scottish player of our time, a splendid footballer who, thanks not least to the swimming exploits of his youth, was far more strongly-built than he might have looked from the terraces or stands. He also had a more than useful turn of foot. He could beat a man, he could use the ball and John thought very highly of his kicking from inside centre. He was not a Scott Hastings in defence but, though

57

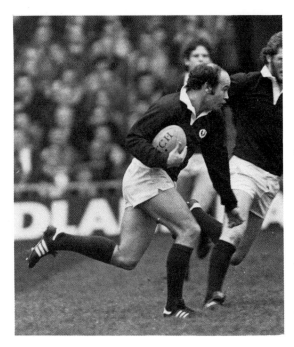

Jim Renwick – a sharp rugby brain

RIGHT
Keith Robertson, a notably versatile footballer. On the right is Alan Tait, now playing Rugby League with Widnes

without that young Watsonian's ability with regard to swift and heavy tackling, he would usually look after even the most exalted of international opponents safely enough. His cover tackling was frequently first-class and informed by a really sharp rugby brain.

His match of matches was the resounding 34-18 defeat of Wales at Cardiff in 1982 in the course of which he not only scored a try but dropped a goal, another of his talents. He was one more player of whom the Lions should have made better use.

He was a humorist even in the cauldron of an international. 'That's the first try I've ever seen live and in slow motion at the same time!' he said to Bruce Hay, as the then Scotland left wing came back upfield after running threequarters of the length of Murrayfield to score against Ireland on an interception.

Renwick was not always wholly in tune with Jim Telfer, least of all when it came to the number and length of Scotland's squad sessions. I have a notion he would have enjoyed himself playing under Carwyn James who was given to catering for

different temperaments and who would even toss Barry John a football and tell him to go and play with it while the others sweated out a more standard session. That said, it should be stressed that Jim Renwick was a great servant to Scotland under Jim Telfer as under other coaches and Jim Telfer was far too shrewd a judge of a player and of a man not to appreciate one of Hawick's favourite sons. Good though Jim Renwick was, John is convinced that he would have been magic if he had played under Ian McGeechan whom more than one knowledgeable pundit reckons to be probably the best coach of backs among the four Home Unions since Carwyn James.

Keith Robertson was very different from Renwick but another grand player in a Scotland jersey. In many ways he was better suited to the wing but, admirably though he often played in that position for Scotland, he did not quite have the pace you look for in that berth.

A versatile footballer who could field beautifully, he did not perhaps kick as well as Renwick but he maybe had the edge as a tackler and he could pass when he chose to do so. Light-footed and uncannily balanced, he could be scintillatingly elusive but was sometimes too individualistic to be everyone's idea of a centre threequarter. The try he scored against England at Twickenham in 1985 has to be one of the best I have seen while John deems him the greatest sevens player he ever knew. No matter what the jersey, John says, 'I'd always pick Keith Robertson at centre and build the rest of the seven round him'.

Up front, Colin Deans and Iain Milne would be contenders for any best-of-all-time Scotland XV, though Milne's selection would depend on just how much store a particular body of selectors put on set scrummaging. Yet he is a much more accomplished all-round forward than many realise. A sound tackler when an opponent is within his orbit, he can use the ball and, as is very obvious on some of the longer runs in training, he can move rather more rapidly than many might think once he is into his stride.

It is, of course, his scrummaging at tight-head which has turned him into a Scottish rugby legend. The other players in the Scotland team, but perhaps myself especially, owe an awful lot more to him than the more casual spectator maybe understands. His power at tight-head, the nudge he could give the scrum, the way he could sometimes drive it back on that flank, must countless times have made my task that much easier whether I was passing, kicking or going on a break.

John will tell you that when the Bear meant business, he could hear him grunting from stand-off and the sound would be music to his ears. Better still, the massive Herioter achieved his effects without infringing the laws by bringing a scrum down or illegally boring. His finest hour, though he would undoubtedly point out feelingly that it lasted a lot longer than that, was the French match at Murrayfield in 1984 when he took some fearful stick but just kept coming back for more.

It was a great pity that he was troubled by injury in the course of the World Cup for he was given all too little chance on the Lions' tour of New Zealand in 1983 and, though he was there with Scotland in 1981, I am not sure that the All Blacks know how good he can be.

Of course, if he had been an All Black himself he would probably be of a rather different shape but at least it has furnished

Iain Milne (on the left) prepares to pack down on Scotland's tight-head with Colin Deans at hooker and David Sole on the loose-head

him with some ammunition for his sense of humour without preventing him from becoming a tremendous force in international rugby. When Scotland had five No. 8s in their pack and the ubiquitously mobile Colin Deans and David Sole in their front row, there was much talk of Scotland having seven glorified flankers, a numerical tag at which Milne pretended to take much umbrage. Similarly, when everyone else was exulting in the perfect conditions represented by a warm and windless afternoon, a dry ball and fast, firm turf, Milne was busy describing the conditions, a twinkle in his eye, as 'Bloody awful!'

Men like the Bear who are characters as well as outstanding players do much to make Rugby Union the game it is and Gavin Hastings, though totally different on both counts, is another who deserves that twin billing. He is faster than he looks, though not exactly fairy-footed on the turn. He has become a fielder to be weighed alongside J. P. R. Williams and he can kick long and far with either foot. With his hefty physique, he can take a lot of stopping, he knows where the enemy try-line is and he has the weight and strength to stand up in the tackle which is integral to much of McGeechan's concept of modern back play.

He can tackle like the proverbial clap of doom but, as Scotland found to their cost last season, he has as yet a weakness when it comes to angling his man against the touchline on his left shoulder. He had a superb World Cup but he seemed a little lighter then, more finely trained, and I think it would pay him to train down a bit from last season's poundage.

As a goalkicker, he can be very long and, when his eye is in, deadly, as witness his haul of eight goals out of eight attempts in the record 33-6 rout of England at Murrayfield in 1986. Nor is he quite as erratic a goalkicker as some allege, though neither there nor in his game as a whole does his consistency yet compare with his potential.

Unusually for a rugby Scot, he gives off a rare air of confidence and even some of that rugby arrogance one was wont to associate with the Welsh. But I would not be too certain that underneath he is quite so sure of himself and as insensitive as many initially suppose.

Gavin Hastings, on paper, should have much of his best rugby still ahead of him but the day of Colin Deans is done, though entirely of his own volition. Had he so chosen, he could have gone on to set a new record for a total of Scottish caps which would have taken some beating.

He must have had plenty going for him from the cradle in respect of guts, determination and competitive zest but, to a great extent, he made himself into the player he was by hard work and practice. He was not even all that skilled a hooker when he began but he became very safe and sure on his own ball in an era when hookers were not expected to win much ball against the head or even to strike for it all that often on the enemy scrum feed. I can readily recall how he would scrum against a goalpost so that he and I could synchronise the put-in and strike, Colin frequently shutting his eyes so that he could, as it were, do it blindfold.

It was the same with his throwing in which, at one stage of his career, he practised endlessly and which he thereafter always kept sharp. Even his exceptional speed about the paddock was not wholly God given for, once he had outgrown the puppy fat

Gavin Hastings, who takes a lot of stopping and who knows where the enemy try-line is

of youth, he spent part of his summers running against the professional sprinters.

His work-rate, especially at the height of his Scotland career, was phenomenal. His tackling, like so much of the rest of his game, mostly succeeded in making light of the fact that he was a bit on the small side, even for a hooker, in the modern game. As you would expect from a Hawick player, who had grown up under Derrick Grant, he knew how to hit a ruck and how to set one up.

His pace, particularly over a short distance, was, however, his greatest asset. Just how quick he at one time became can be gauged from the fact that he and John once had a contest involving sprinting over a short distance and John, as he freely confesses, got the devil of a shock at how difficult Colin was to beat. He was a veritable whirlwind round the front of the lineout. For a spell, he began to take off just too early and put himself out of the game but he soon learned and became again a holy terror on that beat.

By the World Cup, the mileage on the clock was beginning to take its toll. He was not quite as fast as he had been and one had

*Jonathan Davies
of the blazing
acceleration*

the impression that hooking and scrummaging against the much bigger Sean Fitzpatrick in the World Cup quarter-final with the All Blacks really took it out of him. But he was still a great player, much admired in the All Blacks' camp.

Turning to the other countries, John and I were still somewhat naive and inexperienced in international terms when we were on the receiving end of England's 1980 Grand Slam side, and we are not really in a position to pass too much weighty judgement on individuals. But the dazzling running of Clive Woodward, which so split the Scotland defence, will stay with us all our days while a prop like Fran Cotton, who was Test match class on either head on Lions' tours, was obviously a monumental asset. I know that Bill Dickinson, who could be considered an expert on the species, maintained that in all his years he saw none better.

For much of our time England's players were hopelessly hamstrung by inconsistent selection but one whom we would definitely wish to single out was Billy Beaumont. He was not particularly tall by the standards of latter-day lineout specialists and perhaps that was one of the reasons why some down South never seemed to give him his due, at any rate until injury had ended his career and he became in no time at all a folk hero. He was the most honest of workers and an ideal henchman to pack alongside the principal lineout specialist but he was so much more than that.

The nephew of Joe Blackledge, who captained Lancashire in the County Cricket championship, he had good hands as was appropriate to one who was himself very keen on that game and, indeed, at one time this yeoman of England had been a budding full back. His ball-sense showed in the way he used possession and made the ball available, and it also had a lot to do with the fact that Scotland felt he was England's best forward when it came to winning the ball on the floor. To sum up, he was very much the kind of forward you want to give core to your pack.

Our careers did not coincide with a vintage period in Welsh rugby but we both thought very highly of Terry Holmes who, with his physique and strength, was so often a match-winning scrum half even if his service was not to be compared with that of the present incumbent, Robert Jones. Up front, Robert Norster has kept Wales in many a game with his well-timed lineout jumping which, time and again, has given him the upper hand over adversaries several inches taller.

John always maintained that Gareth Davies, a stylish kicker with much of the elegance and thump which the best Welsh stand-offs get into their line-kicking, was a little under-rated but, of course, the stand-off from the Principality on whom he had to keep the most wary of eyes was Jonathan Davies.

Jonathan not only had pace but blazing acceleration as well and once beat John all ends up when John, deep in the Welsh half at Cardiff, came up too straight and fast in endeavouring to pressurize man and ball. After that, John, who seldom made that kind of error twice, came up in defence on a much more balanced and cagier angle.

Like John, Jonathan Davies could turn a game with his penchant for dropping goals and, though a bit variable, he had days when he punted to telling effect, really striking the ball. We always thought that he could tackle, too, though, as with so

'Ollie Campbell was a wonderful kicker from hand and off the deck and, by heaven, he could tackle'

RIGHT
Serge Blanco – a badly placed kick was liable to bring him blazing out of defence

many of the rest of the Welsh, he was made to look very vulnerable in his tackling by the onslaught of the All Blacks in the First Test on Wales's recent venture 'Down Under'.

The Irish had their quota of players of lasting memory such as Phil Orr who was an institution at loose-head prop; Donal Lenihan who did much to remedy a longstanding weakness in the Irish lineout; Philip Mathews, a darned fine flanker; and such backs as Colin Patterson, Tony Ward, Ollie Campbell, Paul Dean and Trevor Ringland.

Patterson, with whom I first tangled at B International level, figured well up my list of enemy scrum halves for whom I had a healthy respect, what with his quicksilver break and an adequate service. Tony Ward at stand-off, though too inclined to jink back inside to be an ideal servant of his threequarters, was an accomplished footballer as might have been expected of one who figured in the same Irish Schools XI as Liam Brady and who later played in European football for Limerick.

In the mind's eye, one can see some lovely flashes from him while Paul Dean delighted many of the stand-offs of yesteryear by the way he committed his own man and got his line away. John believes that the best of Dean is yet to come but, to both of us, the Irish player who stands out above all others against whom we played was Ollie Campbell. He had almost everything, in John's eyes. He had speed, he had hands and he was an adroit and persuasive link from the point of view of the backs outside him. He was a wonderful kicker both from hand and off the deck and, by heaven, he could tackle. His time at the top was sadly cut short and one fears that he will not be accorded quite the place in the game which should be his.

Among the French, who have such strength in depth that it is a minor miracle that Scotland should have beaten them three times in a row at B International level on their own soil, there are players such as Philippe Dintrans, Robert Paparemborde, Pierre Berbizier, Jerome Gallion, Didier Codorniou and Denis Charvet who will feature in many an admiring reminiscence in years to come.

But, for us, the three French players who had that something extra were Jean-Pierre Rives, Philippe Sella and Serge Blanco.

Rives, of the Golden Helmet, as they called that flaxen mane of his, was an insatiable flanker, not all that big but with surprising upper body strength and a selfless, almost technicolour courage. There are miscellaneous pundits who would have it that there are better backs in France than Sella but not to John and me. Very competitive and always prepared to be physical, he is an extra flanker in midfield and yet a glorious threequarter in time-honoured terms. As his hoard of international tries would suggest, he is a lethal finisher.

Serge Blanco was always nominated by John as the most difficult full back against whom he played. In particular, his positioning, wherein he tended to lie unusually wide and close to his open-side wing, made it difficult for even one of John's expertise to use the diagonal, John often feeling it wiser to change his angle and bring the kick infield in a bid to exploit the space Blanco had left. Blanco was richly endowed with both talent and flair and, as was the case when playing against Andy Irvine, one was always uncomfortably aware that a loose or badly placed kick was liable to bring him blazing out of defence.

The Wallabies had a cluster of more than useful backs including Michael Hawker, Michael Lynagh and Brendan Moon but the player who made them tick was indisputably Mark Ella. He had almost supernaturally quick hands and they made all else possible. He had a good left foot for both punting and drop goals and an abundance of intuitive rugby sense, though it should perhaps be said that there were styles of play other than those pursued by the Wallabies in which he would have been a lot less happy and would have looked nowhere near as much of a threat.

It was not so much any very remarkable ability to beat a man which made him dangerous and, in fact, brought him a try in each of the four matches of the Wallabies 1984 Grand Slam in these islands, but rather his exposition of the loop, his running off the ball and his perceptive backing up. A measure of his worth was the rapidity with which the Wallabies fell away after his retirement for, though they were still often formidable, they were not the force they had been.

The Wallabies had their allocation of genuine international forwards but the pick for John and me was unequivocally Mark

An underarm, backhand flip by Mark Ella of the supernaturally quick hands

Loane. He was not notably tall and my recollection is that we won quite a bit of lineout ball from him but he was a terrific No. 8, so strong in both attack and defence. John still winces at the memory of how Loane once ran round him for, as John remarks ruefully, it is one thing to have large forwards endeavouring to run through you but almost insulting when they choose to run round you!

New Zealand's Wayne Shelford is another No. 8 without any great height going for him but, the best forward in the game today, he claims no small amount of lineout ball. Otherwise, even by the All Blacks' demanding standards, he seems close to the complete article, his driving, his defence, his ball-winning and his rucking all fiercely physical and ceaselessly committed. The All Blacks' pack constitute such a homogeneous unit that it is not easy to stand out but Shelford does.

It says much for young Michael Jones at flank forward that he vied with Shelford for the honours in the World Cup. Thrillingly explosive, both on his own account and in support, he had the pace to get out on the enemy midfield, and the number of

Bruce Robertson, who played so persuasively to his wings

RIGHT
John Kirwan – a prolific source of tries

tackles he succeeded in getting in staggered those who, fascinated, began to count them as they watched the television recording. A Mormon whose creed precludes him from playing on Sundays, he is a charming man who took a great trick with the Scots not only as a player but as a person.

Andy Haden was coming to the end of his playing days when John and I came up against him but you could see what a dominating factor he must have been in the lineout. Gary Whetton may not be quite his equal in that dimension but he is, for all that, a lineout jumper whom any team would be glad to own. Simply as a forward, he probably has the edge on Haden. A smashing player to have in the heart of your pack.

Andy Dalton, at hooker, was another All Blacks' forward for whose prowess John and I had a great deal of time, while Sean Fitzpatrick, who played in the World Cup because the All

Blacks' captain was injured, looked every inch the part and made sure that he brought his very considerable physique to bear on the game.

The All Blacks have had so many magnificent back row forwards that it is almost invidious to dwell on one more than another but, having already done so in respect of Shelford and Jones, I cannot leave the forwards without a parting salute to Murray Mexted, the rangy All Blacks' No.8 who caused both Scotland and the Lions some of their most unflattering moments. Hard and athletic, he had in his play, it sometimes seemed to me, more than an echo of Mervyn Davies.

Behind the scrum, as a scrum half myself, I must go first for Dave Loveridge. I played against Australia's John Hipwell but only in the twilight of his career and Loveridge was quite the best scrum half with whom I ever jousted at international or any other level. He had a quick and inviting service born of model footwork. Among his other manifold attributes, nothing was better than the way, when he broke, he had the ball always in two hands and kept it available for the support.

There was class written all over the play of Bruce Robertson, a graceful player who seemed to us almost a throwback to the British centre threequarters of yesteryear in the way in which, as a centre playing outside a first and second five-eighth, he sought to bring his wings into it. Would that we had seen more of him but we saw enough.

Stu Wilson and Bernie Fraser were wings who taught us some very painful lessons, not least in New Zealand in 1981. Neither was easy to bring down. Though Wilson looked more of the thoroughbred, the more obviously pugnacious Fraser was a better runner than perhaps he looked at first sight, the suspicion growing that he was one of those players who is relatively faster in chasing a man or the ball than he is when he has the ball in his hands.

Barely have Wilson and Fraser left the stage than the All Blacks have unearthed John Kirwan, no flying machine but no slouch either. Tall and strongly built, he combines his own versions of the sidestep and swerve with an ability either to break the tackle or stand up in it, his laying off after having made a deep intrusion being a prolific source of tries. He sometimes plays as a forward in sevens and, as John observed, not too many stories illustrate better just how hard and uncompromising the All Blacks are, from front row to full back, than Kirwan's answer when he was asked what he thought of the specialist prop he had been packing against in an international sevens clash.

'To be honest, I thought he was a bit soft. . .'

John Rutherford

4 Self-appraisal

The biggest problems I've had to contend with have usually been presented by fly halfs who attack you. John Rutherford of Scotland is a good example. John is a most difficult opponent. Several times in a match, he will take you on and give you plenty to think about – GARETH DAVIES in his autobiography, *Standing-Off.*

Laidlaw, in particular, is your little terrier, possibly one of the best tackling scrum halfs of all time – ANDY IRVINE in *The Year of the Thistle.*

On our ascent to the representative sphere and, more particularly, the international arena, Roy and I both had a rude awakening in terms of our major technical shortcomings.

For all his break, pugnacity and courage, Roy was uncomfortably aware that his service, which should have been a priority, had been relatively neglected and was sadly inadequate. For my part, though I was far from flawless in other respects, my gravest deficiency lay in the realm of kicking. In my early internationals, I found myself *vis-à-vis* such stand-offs as Gareth Davies of Wales, Tony Ward of Ireland and Bernard Vivies of France, and I was astonished not only by how well they kicked but how powerfully and far.

There was a time, in his later twenties, when Roy was convinced that it was too late for him not so much to learn new tricks as to get out of ingrained bad habits but the 1983 Lions' tour to New Zealand really opened his eyes. Terry Holmes was a great player in his own way, who many a time had used that imposing physique of his to emerge as a match-winner, but his service was no better than Roy's and, indeed, shared some of the same faults. But with the arrival of Nigel Melville, Roy found himself working alongside a scrum half whose major emphasis had always been on a swift service off either hand.

Nigel Melville – an exponent of the swift service off either hand

Roy began to work on his footwork which was an element of British scrum half play which had almost gone out of fashion as lesser mortals wound up in a bid to emulate the huge spin pass of the legendary Gareth Edwards. In 1981, when Scotland were in New Zealand, it was obvious to the shrewder observers in the party that New Zealand scrum halves had not fallen into the same trap for, down through the various levels, they were still getting the rear foot in close proximity to the ball and sweeping the pass away with no preliminary backswing.

Again, where a player like David Kirk, who captained the All Blacks to the World Cup, had worked constantly on his weaker hand, his left, in practice, no-one in his formative years had ever made such a suggestion to Roy. From Melville, though, he learned, by way of a practice device, to pass with one hand, thereby strengthening it much as Henry Cotton used to hit shots one-handed with the same end in mind. In fact, the parallel can be taken further for Cotton hit at least three times as many shots with the left hand alone as he did using just the right though, admittedly, that had as much to do with how he saw the golf swing as with the fact that his right hand was naturally his stronger.

Roy also learned the advantage of practising passing off the left hand with a line of balls hard up against a wall or suitably overturned bench which would preclude that fatal preliminary backswing.

It all helped, of course, and personally I had few complaints concerning his service, especially as no scrum half was ever more reluctant to unload bad ball on to his stand-off than Roy. Nonetheless, Roy will tell you himself that to this day, when passing left to right, he spins the ball off his right or bottom hand rather than doing it correctly with the left. Terry Holmes, Roy noted, did exactly the same.

Turning to my problems with my kicking, it would have been a lot worse but for the erstwhile British Lion and Rugby League player, Ronnie Cowan, for not the least of his contributions to the development of my game had been his insistence on my practising my punting. Even when I was still a schoolmaster, and working as a P E teacher at George Watson's College, I would go out in my lunch hour and kick, with a couple of the keener boys doing the fielding.

However, the point was that I was really not sure on quite what points of technique I should be working. A turning point was the opportunity of practising my kicking with Colin Telfer, a clever tactical kicker himself in his days with Hawick and Scotland, and by then Scotland's assistant coach whose brief was to help out with the backs.

I began to be conscious of a definite improvement but what finally made the difference was my purchase of a video which gave me the chance to study the leading exponents of the contemporary scene in action. The most notable change was probably in the positioning of my hands on the ball. I had always endeavoured to assume the traditional hold with, for a right-footed kick, the ball slanting slightly right to left with the right hand a little on top and the left hand a little below. But,

Roy Laidlaw whips a pass away off his stronger right hand

BELOW
Passing left to right, Roy spins the ball off his right or bottom hand rather than doing it correctly with the left

John demonstrates the grip with which he grew up for a right-footed punt

BELOW
The change of grip for the right-footed punt, which helped to make John into one of the best line-kickers in world rugby

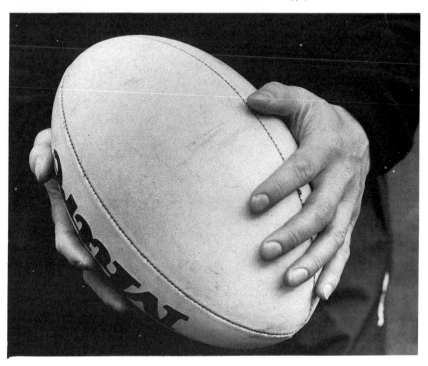

apart from anything else, I was conscious that, at least with me, it took too long to adjust the ball appropriately after taking the pass. Certainly, it was not something I did instinctively.

From my video-tape study of other kickers, I came to the conclusion that I could get the ball much more quickly into position and kick both better and farther if, for a right-footed kick, I held the ball at the same angle but with my right hand under the ball and the left hand advanced simply to steady the hold. It worked at once and somehow the fact that I could now see the whole of the ball did much for my confidence in terms of a flush impact.

For the running diagonal, in which I like to think I eventually became something of a specialist, I held the ball the same way but tilted it down a little more, though the high art of that particular kick lies, of course, in the angle of the foot at impact.

In my earlier days in the Scotland XV, I had neither the assurance nor really the technique to drop for goal but again long hours of practice brought dividends. My grip on the ball was very much the same as for a punt but the release was lower in the sense of being closer to the ground, which I felt cut down the margin for error, my aim being to have the ball pitch on its point and come back just a little. As always, whether punting, dropping goals, or hitting diagonals, I would preface a kick with the right foot with something not far short of a half turn to the right, the exact opposite applying when the boot in question was the left.

If you keep your ears open, you can always learn from other players, past or present. I think I was able to help Richard Cramb by persuading him not to be quite so tucked in when delivering the ball on to his boot for a punt but to give himself more room just as a golfer benefits from a wider arc. Similarly, Australia's Paul McLean was the player from whom I learned to strike the towering up and under on the point of the ball with the hold and delivery virtually vertical. To those who have never tried it, it may sound as if the kick might go anywhere but it is actually very effective with the ball really rocketing skywards.

Roy's own kicking seemed to get better and better, though it is interesting to hear him tracing its evolution. When Roy first

John demonstrating the ball position for a high 'up and under'

OVERLEAF
Roy illustrates the importance for a scrum half of half turning when kicking under pressure

made the South XV, Duncan Paterson, the gifted Gala and Scotland scrum half who was much more than just a great sevens player, underlined the importance for a scrum half of half turning when kicking under pressure in order to hook the ball over the onrushing foe. So many scrum halves, even when kicking from behind a lineout, are very front on which is asking for trouble from the would-be charger-down, especially if he has the rugby sense to aim himself not so much at the kicker but between the kicker and the ball's intended destination. In other words, across the line of flight. It sounds so simple and yet many a match has been lost and won on the ownership or absence of such time-honoured rugby savvy.

Roy's kicking into the box, his probing of the narrow side, had real artistry and timing and not a little of it derived, he always insisted, from the advice of Robin Charters. An international threequarter himself, Charters, a knowledgeable selector who became convener of the S R U selection committee, was at one time a very shrewd coach of the Hawick backs. He was always hammering into Roy that in kicking on the run he must eschew the very real temptation to go just too far and thereby risk having his kick blanketed.

Roy tends to sell himself a little short with regard to what one might describe as midfield passing but he could pass well enough in that guise to perform more than usefully when fielded at stand-off by Jed-Forest. In truth, as wise a rugby man as the late Andrew Bowie of Hawick always believed that Roy would have made a grand stand-off if he had been reared in that role.

I was often criticised, particularly in my earlier seasons with Scotland, for a certain lack of rhythm and style in my passing and much of that comment was well enough founded. I consider I can fairly claim that what I would call my quick passing, the so-called finger-tip stuff, greatly improved and became, in every sense, acceptable. But the classic pass, with the lean away from the recipient which commits a defender, was never my party piece though, together with my passing in general, it came on a lot under Ian McGeechan. We did so much passing of every variety under his tutelage that it would have been difficult for anyone not to get better.

Roy in his version of the classic pass

There are, of course, those who contend that the classic pass is old-fashioned and takes too long but there are plenty of situations in a game of rugby in which it still has a place, not least when players are endeavouring to exploit a numerical overlap, be it three to two, two to one or whatever.

Roy, aside from being a little terrier when it came to spoiling his opposite number, was always a superb player defensively and a wonderfully secure tackler on either shoulder. Even last April, in the sevens, he was to be seen bringing down the like of Hawick's Derek Turnbull a fearful thump.

I could always tackle but I grew up with the notion that stand-offs should really only tackle when there was nothing else for it and that that sort of thing should be down to someone else. It took Jim Telfer about twenty seconds to disabuse me of that view and to instil in me that a stand-off has to be prepared not only to do most of his own defence, and even to pressurize his immediate opponent whenever possible, but also to exploit the countless opportunities afforded by his berth to cover tackle.

In the last few seasons of my career, I did something I would have done long ago if only I had known then what I know now,

which was to set about strengthening my upper body by assid-
uous weight training during the close season. The difference it
made to my confidence was enormous and I took increasing
pride in my defensive contribution. A player like Richard
Cramb, who is an elegant footballer but who could afford to be
a lot more physical in both attack and defence, would surely do
well to learn from my experience.

Roy dive-passing – speed and accuracy more important than length

Robin Charters – a knowledgeable selector whose suggestions helped Roy with his kicking

I had a very bad patch in my career – in fact, there were those clamouring for my omission from the Scotland team – when, under the illusion that I was successfully copying the possibly inimitable Mark Ella, I began to take the ball standing still. Partly because I was a biggish chap for a stand-off, it did not suit me at all, my game lost all its rhythm and the gaps suddenly no longer seemed to be there. Oddly enough, Mark Ella himself greatly surprised me when I raised the matter with him for he was adamant that he never took the ball standing still but was always, at least to a degree, on the move.

That said, I was never any good at blazing on to the scrum half's pass as Colin Telfer would have liked me to do. Latterly, Roy would not pass so much in front of me, which had sometimes led to a tendency for me to drift across field, but more directly at me so that, although I was moving on to the pass, I was running straight.

Roy, even when his service had greatly improved, would still have sided with the Irish and Lions' scrum half, Andy Mulligan, who long ago declared that 'A huge pass requiring a countdown and liquid oxygen for fuel is useless.' Like his great hero and old adversary, the All Blacks' Dave Loveridge, Roy was much more intent on speed and accuracy and, for all that his service had its critics to the very end of his international days, I had better cause than anyone to appreciate its merits.

Promisingly though Jed-Forest are now shaping, Roy played much of his earlier career in club rugby behind beaten forwards and learned to live on his wits. Whereas an All Blacks' scrum half such as Loveridge or Kirk is usually not going to have to deal with the ball until it has been nicely laundered by the pack, Roy had frequently either to dig it out for himself amid grasping enemy paws or somehow get an untidy ball safely away amid opponents' flying feet.

It helped him as well as me, of course, that our understanding became telepathic, for a stand-off can ease the lot of his scrum half only less than vice versa. Nor did that understanding manifest itself only in attack, for in defence, when I was already committed to one or other side of the scrum, ruck or maul, I could call to him to take my man if that worthy went the other way.

Positionally, we both learned much along the way. Roy in the later years stationed himself much closer to the front of the lineout so that he would be moving on to the ball in the direction in which he wanted to pass. Again, he also stayed within three metres or so of the lineout in order that if the delivery from the forwards were loose, he would be already moving away from the enemy as he sought to retrieve it and get it away rather than moving forward into their maw.

Similarly, I picked up from Mark Ella and the Wallabies' coach, Alan Jones, the practice of basically stationing myself opposite the end man in their lineout. This meant that, if I took Roy's pass running straight, the breakaway was going to find it much more difficult to police me and still move easily out on to my centres.

Obviously, not every half-back partnership is going to enjoy the luxury of more than eighty representative games together but ideally, if assorted selectors give them a real chance to fuse, the sum of the whole should be greater than the individual parts. Perhaps that is one claim we could make without any danger of being accused of boasting!

5 Captains of different hues

At five feet seven inches, Roy Laidlaw may be the smallest man in Scotland's line-up against Ireland on Saturday but his team-mates will tell you he has by far the biggest heart – BRIAN MEEK *in the* Daily Express, January 1983.

John Rutherford looked very much the part. He was one of the very few Lions' backs who was capable of taking on the defence – a lovely, balanced runner and, in these barren times of kicking fly halfs, something of a throwback to more imaginative days – KARL JOHNSTON IN *The Lions of Winter.*

In the domain of senior rugby, Roy and I both have some depth of experience in the matter of captaining sides. Both of us led our club sides, Selkirk in my case, Jed-Forest in Roy's, to promotion from Division II to Division I and each in our time has captained the South to a Grand Slam in the Inter-District championship.

Roy captained Scotland on five occasions, his matches in charge being spread on either side of the 1984 Grand Slam. None was won and that fact, to my possibly not entirely unbiased eye, has all too readily been allowed to obscure the fact that Roy had a great deal of what it takes to make a very good international captain.

He himself says that, though he relished the honour and never felt that captaining a team in itself adversely affected his own play, he rather lost confidence in himself in that role as defeat followed defeat.

There were, nevertheless, very definite mitigating circumstances. I myself played in only one of Roy's quintet of games as captain which, whatever else it meant, entailed Roy having to divert part of his attention to linking with a less familiar partner. If that was no help to Roy, much worse was the fact that in neither season in which he captained his country was Jim Telfer in charge and, in those earlier years in the eighties, there was apt to be all the difference in the world between Scotland with Jim Telfer and Scotland without.

We werè just emerging on the international scene in the closing years of the careers of Ian McLauchlan, who captained Scotland a record nineteen times, and of Mike Biggar who led his country after being groomed for the post at B international level, and on Scotland's 1977 tour of the Far East, the latter a venture on which both Roy and I went.

I cannot truly say that I really remember McLauchlan tactically. The impression he left on both of us was of a captain ruthlessly and ferociously committted to the cause, who was no mean motivator and who used his long experience at Scotland and Lions' level to detail with much accuracy the strengths and weaknesses of many of our leading opponents.

Mike Biggar was a very different kind of man but he, too, was in love with rugby; a thoroughly honest forward who made the very most of what he had and who always set a fine example by his own selfless industry.

Jim Renwick never captained Scotland – mostly, I suspect, because he never particularly coveted the post. But though perhaps a somewhat reluctant captain, he was a darned good one who, if he was landed with the responsibility, put his heart and soul into it and was tactically brilliant.

Ian McGeechan, as you would expect of one who was to develop into such a great coach, knew the game inside out. He had a way with players, who respected him both as a man and as a player. One little touch I well remember came in my international debut against Wales at Murrayfield in 1979.

The wind was sweeping almost straight down the pitch and McGeechan came to me, a complete newcomer to the full international arena, and asked me which way I would prefer to play if he won the toss. 'With the wind,' I replied and, sure enough, we had that wind at our backs in the first half as I sought to settle into the match and get my international career off on the right foot.

Andy Irvine, as Roy and I agree, made an almost perfect foil

Andy Irvine – tactically he was always instinctively geared to attack and so often, too, he was a match-winning goalkicker

to Jim Telfer as coach when captaining Scotland to New Zealand in 1981 and to Australia in 1982. Both were great enthusiasts, who could be very passionate about their rugby but Andy Irvine's dashing personality balanced Jim Telfer's then somewhat brooding intensity.

To a comparatively young player such as myself, Andy was a positive inspiration while tactically he was always instinctively geared to attack. Moreover, he knew how to exploit the panoramic view of the exchanges behind the scrum which a full back enjoys and never seemed to mind or bear any malice when an over-zealous suggestion was somewhat colourfully and abruptly rejected by a stand-off with more pressing matters immediately to hand.

As for Jim Aitken, there is a tendency to denigrate his contribution as captain to the Grand Slam but Roy and I do not go along with that. True, with a coach like Jim Telfer, who not only has a very strong personality but who thinks of everything, the captaincy is hardly the almost all-embracing job it was when Jim Telfer was, to all intents and purposes, Scotland's captain and coach all rolled into one. But no-one knew better than Telfer that there was a vital part for Jim Aitken to play and that he played it well.

Telfer, in fact, was wont to point to the difference Jim Aitken had made to Gala, reflecting that they had often had the players to win the Scottish championship but had not done so since 1931-2 until Jim Aitken drove, led or cajoled them into a cohesive, winning unit. On the New Zealand tour of 1981, his faith in Jim Aitken as a scrummaging coach was early in evidence. When Aitken captained Scotland to the resounding defeat of Canterbury which Telfer still rates the best performance by any Scotland team under his coaching command, a significant step, though one did not know it at the time, was taken on the road which culminated in the championship triumphs of 1984.

Aitken's detractors even used to assert that he was not good enough as a loose-head prop, snorting that when he was in trouble he either brought the scrum down or broke away too easily from his hooker and popped up out of the scrum, compelling the referee to begin the whole thing all over again. One would have to admit that one sometimes heard Colin Deans

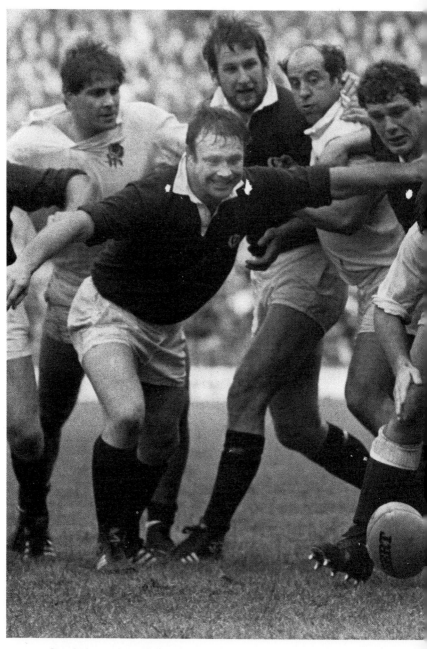

Jim Aitken – the confidence he exuded was very important in a small rugby nation such as Scotland

urging him not to come away from him, but the fact remains that Aitken played against some outstanding tight-head props in his day, men like Price of Wales and Paparemborde of France, and neither Roy nor I can remember his really having damagingly the worse of it. Roy, for the record, has said that, as the scrum half providing the feed, he always felt that Scotland's ball was very secure in those years when Jim Aitken was helping Colin Deans to lock up the Scotland loose-head.

Aitken, Roy used to observe to me, had the great advantage of seeming very confident in his ability both as a player and as a captain. But then he is that kind of personality, a remarkable bloke who in his time has acted as a ballroom bouncer in Penicuik and yet who is today the director of several companies.

He made an admirable lieutenant to Jim Telfer both on and off the field. The confidence he exuded was very important in a small rugby nation such as Scotland who, for all too long in the post-war years, were competing against an inferiority complex as much as their opponents.

By astute and diligent weight training, Aitken built up his physique and was always very fit. Some pointed to a tendency to fringe rather more than many another international prop but that very tendency to stand back and have a look may have actually assisted him in his tactical appraisal. Roy always admired how clear cut and decisive he was in calling the shots at a lineout and, though it barely proved necessary in the course of the Grand Slam, he was one of those captains – and there are not that many of them – who could change tactics in the course of a game amid the thudding heat of battle.

Roy always concludes any argument on Aitken as a captain by simply stating that he can stand on his record; a record which includes the 1983 Calcutta Cup match, which was only Scotland's second win at Twickenham in the post-war years, when Aitken took over the captaincy from Roy and, according to Roy, led the side excellently.

Roy's other successor in his two spells of captaincy was David Leslie whose brief reign would have been marked by a win at Twickenham in 1985 but for a capricious bounce of the ball under the England posts.

David was very intelligent and a most accomplished player

Jean-Pierre Rives – technicolour courage

Colin Deans, who led by example, has an encouraging word for Derek White with Iain Paxton listening in

who, psyched up for an international, was indisputably one of the greats of Scottish rugby, but he was also something of a man apart and at times a bit of a loner. The international stage was very much his scene but in the bread and butter weeks of the club season he was not perhaps always on quite the same wavelength as the other Scotland players.

They respected him hugely as a player but were possibly a little wary of him as a man, while his own total commitment and involvement would not have helped him to take the larger view tactically. However, if the captaincy had come to him at a different juncture of his career, it might all have worked out very differently for him.

Not the least of the strengths of Colin Deans as a captain was that he so savoured the office. At first, he perhaps went a little too far. Where Jim Telfer, as coach, would sometimes use his fist to give some massive forward a dig or punch in the final pre-match build-up to the physical explosion that is the frontal battle in a modern international, Colin would give backs and forwards alike a not altogether playful slap across the face.

The senior players soon got together and had a word with him and, to his credit, he at once dispensed with the practice without sacrificing anything of his ability to motivate his troops. Tactically, his Hawick upbringing had left him with the deepest distrust of backs who failed to keep the ball in front of the forwards, the carrot in front of the donkey, but normally he was content to leave most of the tactical decisions in the hands of myself and Roy who, whatever else we may have lacked, were certainly not short on experience.

What made Colin the captain he was, and judged overall he was pretty successful, was the ability to lead by example. He was such a terrific player, so swift about the field as to act almost as a pacemaker for the rest of his forwards. The way he sailed into the tackle and hit rucks was more inspiringly eloquent than any amount of words.

With only one full cap behind him, it was not easy for Gary Callander to take over the reins of captaincy from such a world-famous personality as Colin Deans, and the loss of other key personnel did not help him either. He long ago demonstrated with Kelso that he is a natural leader and again one of that small band of captains who are not only sound in their planning before a match but who have either the feel or vision, if not both, to make important tactical switches in mid-match.

Among the other nations, Andy Dalton of the All Blacks was always ranked by Roy and me among the finest captains against whom we played – one of those captains whose grip on his team and the game penetrated to the opposition. Jean-Pierre Rives and Philippe Dintrans had something of the same quality. When Rives spoke, you could sense his players really zooming in on what he had to say, while I remember an afternoon when Dintrans was at the core of France's short penalty moves. With his pack behind him, one got a graphic close-up of the leadership he was giving them, the example he was setting.

I played both with and against Billy Beaumont and always found him a very good captain who knew what he wanted and generally got it, and again his own play provided a stirring lead. Ciaran Fitzgerald took an awful lot of flak when captaining the Lions in New Zealand in 1983 but at least some of his troubles were not of his making and Roy and I both always think of him as a darned good captain of Ireland. Whatever his detractors say, his record with Ireland speaks for itself and, talking to the Irish players, it was clear that they liked and admired him.

I share also with Roy the belief that the captain should best be from among the front nine, but that if he is a forward, and especially a member of the tight five, he needs one or more of his inside backs to have vision and a tactical awareness and authority. It is an interesting exercise to think back to some of the great captains from the front row or lock and realise just how fortunate they were in that regard. Try it for yourself.

Of course, a man can be a born leader irrespective of where he plays and frequently, for all the reservations imposed by his berth, he will still be the obvious and correct choice. Before I leave that particular subject, people often comment with some surprise on the number of hookers who have made their mark as captains. For my own part, I take the point that in most games there are more lineouts than scrums and that therefore at the main set-piece the hooker is more often cast as a glorified blind-side flanker than buried amid the rival packs' locked antlers.

A captain has to be respected. Ideally, he should be an outstanding player but, if he is not, he must still be worth his place and held in high esteem for his own commitment. As previously implied, he should have vision. If he does not, it is imperative that he has a lieutenant in a key berth, probably among the four inside backs and preferably at scrum half or stand-off, who has that priceless ingredient.

Even today, when the advent of coaches at club and representative level and a better back-up from the selectors and company take some of the old responsibilities off the captain's shoulders, he still has a great part to play off the field as well as on it. The ability to inspire others with the spoken word comes in many guises and match-winning orations have varied from just a few telling words to speeches to be bracketed with Shakespeare's Henry V at Agincourt and Winston Churchill's in the darkest hours of the last war.

Nor, for captains no less than for coaches, does a sense of humour come amiss, for it is often at the most emotional and emotive moments that a rugby player's impish levity is liable to manifest itself. One can think of innumerable instances but would cite just one. That pre-match call to battle when Nairn MacEwan, as Scotland's coach, was endeavouring to work the Hawick and Scotland lock, Alan Tomes, up to a proper pitch for an encounter with Wales. Having gone on at some length about the bloodcurdling things which Geoff Wheel would do to him at lineout after lineout, MacEwan paused dramatically and asked, 'And what will you do about it?'

Tomes was a tough enough hombre not to have to bother about mock heroics. 'I'll let him have all the ball he wants. . .'

Which was not quite the answer for which Nairn was looking.

6 Learning from other countries
The cockerel, kiwi and kangaroo

*John Rutherford was the one Lions' back of 1983 who would slot into an
All Black team. A beautiful rugby player, every skill, he can turn the game
around with individual brilliance –* STU WILSON and BERNIE FRASER
in *Ebony and Ivory.*

*Scotland swung the Canterbury scrum against the head. Laidlaw bril-
liantly intercepted Steve Scott's pass and sped in for a try. Not for nothing
was Laidlaw later congratulated on his game by Bill Dalley, one of the
few survivors from the 1924 Invincibles –* NORMAN MAIR on Canterbury *v.* Scotland, May 1981, in the *Sunday Standard.*

For all the All Blacks' unequivocal victory in the World Cup,
John and I both thought that there were an awful lot of rugby
folk around the world who did not realise how good they were.
But, if the Scotland squad were anything to go by, the players
always knew.

So many seemed to insist on regarding them as ruthlessly
and relentlessly efficient but little more than so many programmed robots. Yet after three successive encounters with
Wales, in which the try-score was an awesome 26-2 in the All
Blacks' favour, even their most cynical denigrators must have
begun to suspect that there might be a thing or two to learn
from them.

As the New Zealanders themselves have long noted,
Scotland, thanks chiefly to Jim Telfer, have been the home
country most anxious to model their game on the All Blacks.
Telfer, of course, has an All Black's belief in the ruck but he was
also shrewd enough to realise that it was likely to be much
better suited to the material at his disposal than the maul.

It might be different for an England pack with the size born of their numerical strength and with so many forwards with a great deal of upper body strength. For the Scots, a rucking rather than mauling game made sense because getting there quickly in numbers and hitting the ruck in concert, with good technique, could more than offset the physical advantage of larger but perhaps heavier-footed enemy forwards.

Though no nation in rugby terms are better at staying on their feet than New Zealand, and they are the best ruckers of all, some of the laws designed to stop players going to ground and laying the foundation of a sterile pile-up have actually encouraged certain teams to maul in situations where once they would have rucked. But the All Blacks have merely adapted their methods to make their driving up front still more lethal without lessening the impact of their rucking. Iain Paxton played in the World XV against Australia in Sydney in connection with the home nation's Bicentennial celebrations and, besides coming to the conclusion that Wayne Shelford was the best player with whom he had ever shared a rugby field, was struck by how devastatingly they had turned the changes in the laws in their favour.

They did not put the ball on the ground and ruck over it as early as he had expected but rather fought to stay on their feet and turned to look for support to drive still farther into the entrails of the beleaguered defence before delivering a superb ball to the backs from a rucking pack still driving dynamically forward. With those words of Paxton's in mind, one watched on television the annihilation of the Welsh with a more knowledgeable and appreciative eye.

In 1981, when more than one revered New Zealand pundit congratulated Jim Telfer on Scotland's rucking, and suggested that the wearers of the thistle would consequently carry all before them in the coming International Championship, Jim explained ruefully that, back home, the interpretations of the referees were so different that Scotland would not be allowed to take up in the Five Nations championship where they had left off Down Under. Apart from anything else, in New Zealand rugby the referee's sympathies tend to lie less with the man killing the ball than with those reminding him of

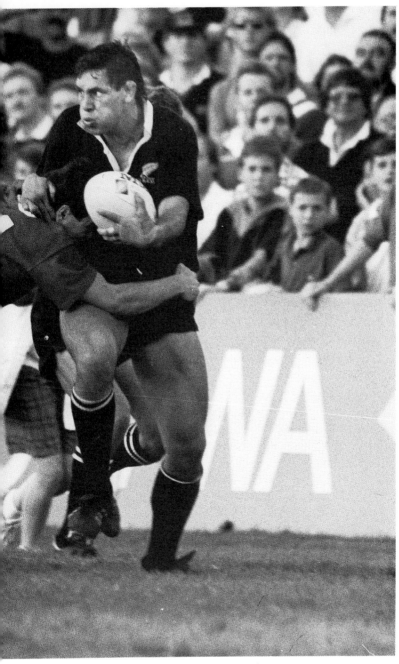

Wayne Shelford – the best forward in the game today

the error of his ways, always providing they do not go too far.

None the less, with those reservations, the ruck has to remain integral to the Scotland pattern. After all, the ruck has been at the very heart of Scotland's style in the eighties, and the eighties have been Scotland's most rewarding period since the twenties.

John and I both understand, from old players whose opinions we respect, that Scotland's collective work in the scrum was often very poor, almost from the coming of specialisation with regard to set positions in the scrummage until quite far into the post-war years. The S R U, or at any rate their selectors, were seemingly very slow to grasp that specialisation had come to stay or that the 3-4-1 scrum was an advance on the 3-2-3, save for given manoeuvres such as the old-fashioned but still, as late as the sixties, sometimes effective, wheel and dribble.

Scotland's first coach, Bill Dickinson, soon established himself as the High Priest of the set scrum but, even before his day, there had reputedly been a marked improvement, with the advent of such outstanding prop forwards as Hugh McLeod, David Rollo, Sandy Carmichael and Ian McLauchlan, to name but four.

Dickinson, though, in the annals of Scottish rugby, will be as indelibly associated with the scrummage as Telfer is with the ruck and his legacy is arguably the emphasis Scotland still place on scrummaging to this day. France and England, among the sides in the International Championship, have also mounted some formidable scrummaging units in the recent past but, just as long as Iain Milne was there as the cornerstone of the pack, the Scotland backs always felt pretty confident that the forwards would hold their own or more in the set scrum.

At least since the coming of the hindmost foot off-side law, it is much easier for the backs to attack off first phase from the set scrum than from the lineout. The stress on getting the scrummaging right, the time spent on it particularly on the additional Wednesday evening squad sessions for the Scotland forwards, is eminently worthwhile but there are two points which should be made.

In the first place, particularly since the success the 1984

Wallabies had using the Powerhouse scrummaging machine, there has been a temptation to neglect live scrummaging against another pack of forwards. That form of practice is, of course, much closer to the real thing and it was illuminating to hear John tell of how, way back in 1979, the All Blacks' hooker, Andy Dalton, had spoken of the importance they attach to that mode of scrummaging preparation.

The second point is again something we can learn from the All Blacks. It is always said that they regard the set scrum only as a means of restarting the game but, vulnerable though they evidently were in this sphere in the early seventies, they invariably seem nowadays to find forwards who are not only entirely adequate as scrummagers but redoubtable all-round forwards. To put it another way, you don't find them picking a forward solely on his scrummaging as often happens in the Five Nations championship. In truth, the silhouette of some of the more portly tight forwards in Europe would look almost laughably out of place in an All Black's strip.

When it comes to the lineout, Scotland in our time have frequently been dangerously small and light. The powers-that-be can't grow towering locks to order but they can play a telling part in the grooming of such big men as we have – and, just as John and I are bowing out, there are suddenly some lofty fellows about with Damian Cronin having wasted scant time in making a considerable impression on the international arena.

Of necessity, Scotland learned to make enterprising use of what lineout assets we did possess – such as two outstanding throwers-in in Colin Deans and Gary Callander and a lineout tail-gunner capable of real brilliance in David Leslie.

In the World Cup, New Zealand and France should have taught us something else: that there is still a place for a player very much akin to the open-side wing forward of yesteryear. In the World Cup final, Michael Jones, as Andy Haden wisely observed in the radio commentary, was so quick about the field he was constantly putting pressure on the French midfield, the effect of which was felt all along the line. In contrast, with no Jean-Pierre Rives to call upon now, the French back row were made to look almost leaden-footed because of the absence of pace at flank forward.

Andy Dalton – All Black hooker and a great captain who was an advocate of live scrummaging practice. On his right, at tight-head, is Gary Knight and on his loose-head, John Ashworth

Both John and I much prefer to have our flankers playing open and blind rather than left and right, though plainly a lot can hinge on the particular attributes of the players available. John says that he was always conscious of playing under much more pressure when there was a genuine open-side wing forward ranged against him, citing Ireland's Nigel Carr as a notable example. John, in fact, sees advantages even today in playing your open-side always on that flank at a set scrum, especially as he reckoned that it greatly simplified his own defensive role as a stand-off.

In my own berth of scrum half, I realised almost the moment I set foot Down Under that the occupants of the No.9 jersey on that side of the world were far ahead of most of the scrum halves in Europe in the way they swept the pass away in a single movement with no backswing. The action was made possible by sound, positive positioning and exemplary footwork.

As John was recalling in a recent rugby conversation, the Lions on occasion would take provincial teams apart but, on the whole of that 1983 tour of New Zealand, we never saw a bad scrum half. No matter how adverse the circumstances, it seemed that they could always cope. I gather that at Under-19 level and below, the opposing scrum half is not allowed to advance beyond a line drawn through the mouth of the scrum tunnel until the ball is out. Though I know there are two opinions on that even in New Zealand, I can see how it would give an up-and-coming scrum half the opportunity to work on his footwork and technique as opposed to having to get the ball away anyhow with the enemy hounding him.

Like John, I long ago came round to preferring the New Zealand formation wherein they play a first and second five-eighth inside a centre, rather than our time-honoured midfield of a stand-off and centres playing left and right. Many back divisions in this country who do play an inside and outside centre have actually missed much of the point, which is that the partnership and understanding between a first and second five-eighth can matter as much as that between half backs. In New Zealand, just as the papers in Britain used to say how often John and I had played together, they will give a similar statistic for the two five-eighths.

Dave Loveridge – the best scrum half against whom Roy played and from a land where those who wear the No. 9 jersey are far ahead of the majority of scrum halves in Europe

John played a Test match at second five-eighth for the Lions and always maintained that, given an extended run in the position, he would have come to enjoy it just as much as he did stand-off. That one pass more – the pass from the first five-eighth to the second – can make such a difference even in terms of kicking, with different angles and the opposing defence already that little bit more committed.

The second five-eighth, alias the inside centre, has a crucial role to play in straightening the running of the back division, though that is not to say that the stand-off does not also have a key part to play in that realm. John thinks that both the Australians and the French, at their best, were in a class of their own in our time in running straight, but that Scotland improved over the seasons.

He is an admirer, too, of the Wallaby alignment wherein the first five-eighth, second five-eighth and centre often lay quite tight and flat, thereby making it much harder for the men marking them to adopt a drift defence. That deployment of the midfield was supplemented by the other threequarters and full back coming from depth and hitting the attack at pace.

The other side of that card was the way the French backs would often align so steeply that a drift defence was absolutely essential, because the worst thing you could do against them was to sell yourself in midfield by rushing at them headlong in a forlorn attempt to take man and ball together.

Another view John and I have in common is that both Wallaby and All Blacks' wings are far better than most of those in Europe at finding a way into the action. The manner in which Stu Wilson and Bernie Fraser materialised in the line from blind-side wing, often quite far out, caused us all kinds of trouble on Scotland's 1981 tour to New Zealand. What is more, not only do they come off their regular beat in search of work or sudden intrusion much more readily but both the Australian and the New Zealand wings are streets ahead in their use of the ball and in the way they set it up and present it with regard to the support.

Where full backs are concerned, Scotland have been blessed in the last decade with Andy Irvine and Gavin Hastings, both in their different ways match-winners. Full backs of their calibre give you so many attacking options.

John recognises better than most the possibilities opened up by having a stand-off with real pace, especially off the mark. Yet, at the same time, he hazards that stand-off could be the one berth behind the scrum in which you could still get away with a comparatively slow runner. Otherwise he thinks that, among the backs, pace everywhere is nowadays close to mandatory at international level. He is right, too, for when you play the like of the Wallabies or the Tricolors, the speed of foot they sometimes have within their ranks can be really intimidating.

It is not just on the field itself that we can learn from other rugby nations. The level of fitness attained by the All Blacks is a major factor in their recent record and not for nothing is it said that Jim Blair, the expatriate Scot who is their trainer, did as

Stu Wilson, who taught us some very painful lessons

much to win the World Cup as one player.

He is paid for his services and, before that World Cup, a squad of sixty players, later suitably reduced, were individually assessed and then given conditioning programmes tailored to each man's position on the field and particular physical requirements. Blair and his colleagues have three separate clinics spread throughout New Zealand and the progress of the players on the squad was regularly monitored.

We have a ready-made Jim Blair in our physiotherapist, Dave McLean, but I am afraid the S R U would have to swallow hard and draw a deep breath before enlisting the services of a paid trainer. Yet such a man could have much to offer at every level of the game, particularly if he were as steeped in his craft and as enthusiastic as McLean. John and I both consider that such an appointment has to come but fear that it may not be for many a day.

In a splendid article in the *Sunday Times*, Stephen Jones reiterated Gary Whetton's reminder that even in New Zealand the forwards nowadays are not all farmers or manual labourers. As Blair said on his winter visit to his native land, the picture of the All Blacks' forwards at home on their farms with a sheep under each arm was perhaps always something of a myth but it is now totally erroneous. Nevertheless, as he said, they are still an outdoor people by comparison with most other nationalities and they will, for instance, do their own concreting, put up their own fences, rather than send for professional assistance.

Be all that as it may, they understand that now that so many of them have somewhat softer jobs by comparison with the farmers and manual labourers of past years, they must work harder than ever on their conditioning through progressive weight training and so forth.

Jones told of how Whetton has four separate programmes for his pre-season work. Basic, Weights, Explosive and Rugby Skills. He monitors his own blood-oxygen levels and his body-fat ratio and comments, 'The main thing is to understand what is happening to your body and to realise that there is no way out, no help. You have to put the work in yourself.'

If an All Black of Whetton's calibre finds all that necessary, it is probably trebly so for so many less enviably endowed

Gary Whetton – a phenomenal athlete by traditional lock forward standards

forwards in Scotland and elsewhere.

Blair underlined the use New Zealanders make of the close season in respect of their physical fitness, playing other sports in the first two months by way of a change to keep them fresh, and then concentrating for the next three months on flexibility, endurance and strength. Think of the basis which all that has already given them before they get down to serious in-season work. Additionally, New Zealand rugby players are far more prepared to train and practise on their own outside the club and representative squad sessions. Very slowly, I feel, players in Scotland are beginning to get the message.

The World Cup did wonders for the game in New Zealand which not so long before had been badly damaged by a spate of

David McLean, the S R U physiotherapist, treating Scott Hastings. McLean has much to offer to every level of the game

serious injuries – something partly countered by changes in the laws – and by the visit of the Springboks which split not just the country but even families.

Their marketing, in terms of the follow-up, has been something to witness, the seeds sown long before the first ball was kicked in the World Cup. To give one striking example, a video was prepared which took in everything: the All Blacks' preparation, individual interviews with players, how they saw the opposition and their interpretation of their own berths, almost everything you could think of.

Armed with that kind of aid, John Kirwan, the great All Blacks' wing, is apparently employed by the Auckland Rugby Union to sell the game both in the schools and outside them.

The S R U have always disliked the cult of the personality

and have seen rugby strictly as a team game, one favourite anecdote of many an after-dinner speaker being of how at Twickenham in 1928 King George V asked the S R U's J. Aikman Smith why the Scotland players were not numbered and received the tart reply, 'Sir, this is a rugby match, not a cattle market.'

Just as the S R U have moved on from that memorable exchange so both John and I fervently believe that if Scottish rugby is to overcome the dire effect of the industrial trouble in the schools – which saw the number of boys playing drop from 15,000 to under 5000 – 'name' players will have to be used to sell the game on lines not so very different from the job Kirwan is doing with Auckland.

The S R U Youth Marketing Committee, under Freddie McLeod, the former Stewart's College F P full back, has already done some good work, not least with the Youth Open Days at Murrayfield and at Rubislaw in Aberdeen. But the number of boys playing, though increasing, is still alarmingly far below the number before the aforesaid industrial trouble and clearly much more has to be done.

When we were in Australia in 1982, we saw what curtain-raisers before a big match could do to catch the imagination of the young, our two Tests being preceded by the Australian Under-21 XV meeting, respectively, their Fijian and New Zealand counterparts.

We both greatly like the suggestion that club matches in Scotland should be prefaced by an Under-14 curtain-raiser perhaps of only twelve-a-side and twenty minutes each way duration. We are sure also that Hawick are on to something with their Under-16 team who are coached on Sunday mornings by Colin Deans and a combination of the club coaches and leading players.

Above all, let Scotland take a leaf from the Silver Fern and, with the next World Cup already looming, take the game to the nation's youth.

7 Great coaches

Jim Telfer – an iron fist in an iron glove

There was the controlled poise of those marvellous half backs, Laidlaw and Rutherford, one of the great double acts in Scottish rugby history – CLEM THOMAS *in the* Observer, March 1987.

I've always had great respect for Rutherford and Laidlaw, but it has grown after this game – MICK DOYLE, *Irish coach, on Scotland v. Ireland 1986.*

I was in the Scotland squad before the end of Bill Dickinson's long reign as the Scotland coach and John had him as his club coach at Selkirk. Thus, between us, we have had first hand experience of all those who have coached Scotland to the end of the 1988 International Championship.

Those who played in the early seventies have underlined that Dickinson had no easy task, because he was being called upon to break new ground in Scotland. To the traditionalists, at least as far as senior rugby was concerned, in marked contrast to their attitude to school rugby, coach was one of the nastiest 'five-letter' words in the English language. The very fact that his title was no more than that of 'Adviser to the Captain' spoke of the need to appease some of the older brigade. Nor was it necessarily a coincidence that Dickinson was not himself an international because that made it that much less likely that he would rapidly develop into the kind of supremo the S R U dreaded. Not that, with coaching in most of the clubs still on a very unofficial level, they had too many proven claimants from whom to choose.

A further grumble with which he had to contend was that not everyone in Scottish rugby had approved of Jordanhill's style of rugby under him. They had very much played to their strength which was a well-drilled and abrasive pack supported by some excellent kicking by their half-backs, much of it from stand-off by John Roxburgh, nowadays the S R U's senior technical administrator.

Dickinson was under no illusions but I should doubt if he would have coveted any post in the world, from President of the USA to Principal of Loughborough, more dearly. He was essentially a forwards' coach with his special subject the set scrum. With Ian McLauchlan, from his Jordanhill pack, as his man in the field, he turned the Scotland scrum into a unit which on more than one occasion proved a match-winning weapon. Some, particularly among the Welsh, saw all the deliberate screwing, slewing and crabbing of the scrum as very negative. Yet, especially in conjunction with as deadly a spoiler as Douglas Morgan from scrum half, it could be terribly awkward to play against, as even the incomparable Gareth Edwards found to his cost.

It was generally accepted that Dickinson did little coaching of the backs but accusations concerning the extent to which he was supposed to have inhibited them were often unfair and denied by many of the outsides who played under him in a Scotland jersey. For instance, the Scotland back division when he came in, back in 1971, had some excellent performers including the inside quartet with Duncan Paterson and Jock Turner at half-back and the darting acceleration of Chris Rea alongside the strapping John Frame in the centre. They had a great respect for Dickinson and were convinced that he had helped them not so much by coaching as by what he did for the team in which they operated as a whole.

He has been in demand all over the world from a country steeped in rugby such as New Zealand to an emergent rugby nation like the Portuguese. In his seventies, he was still helping out at Burnbrae last season, while he was already well into his sixties when he coached Selkirk. The way in which he was prepared to travel from his home in Glasgow to Philiphaugh sometimes three times in one week made a deep impression on the Selkirk players who were lost in grateful admiration for his dedication. Two cars, containing Dickinson and Selkirk players, would do the leg from Edinburgh to Selkirk and, for all the Borderers' appetite for rugby, the players who travelled down with Dickinson were not those who travelled back with him, simply because the intensity of his rugby talk was too much for any of them to take both ways.

He knew all about his own image and, I have a notion, rather mischievously enjoyed living up to it. Probably well aware that it would be repeated in clubhouses all over the country, he told the Selkirk players that when he took off his faithful old cap, it was a signal for them 'to tighten up the game and not let the ball out beyond the scrum half.' It was John from whom I first heard that tale and another he used to love to relate was of Dickinson's parting words to the Selkirk team before one match: 'Now I want you to get stuck in, really stuck in, to the point where I can turn to my neighbour in the stand and exclaim, "If I had known Selkirk were as rough as this, I'd never have agreed to coach them".'

Dickinson's successor, Nairn MacEwan, was to win only one match before retiring from the Scottish international scene with heart trouble. But, if only he had not acceded to the post too soon, how different it might have been, for both John and I are convinced that he could have been a truly notable coach had he but served a proper apprenticeship first. He had been a memorable player for Scotland at flank forward and that should have got him off to a good start with regard to having the respect of the players. But the trouble was that he was too close to them and, when things started to go wrong, there were murmurings that he did not realise that what had worked for Highland, in their climb up the ladder represented by the national leagues, was frequently not applicable in the harsh reality of the international stage.

That was the main criticism made of him – that he was not a realist. Without disagreeing, John and I would put it another way, pointing out that he was a little unlucky in not really having the players to play his type of game. Following his controversial suspension after being sent off for retaliation in an Inter-District match at Murrayfield, Gordon Brown never played for Scotland again and he left a void in the Scotland pack which badly damaged MacEwan's prospects as a coach.

118

The Scotland team who toured the Far East in 1977 and who were coached by Nairn MacEwan. Back row (left to right): Roy Laidlaw, Colin Deans, John Rutherford, Rob Moffatt, Keith Robertson, Malcolm Hurst, Jock Berthinussen, Lewis Dick. Middle row: Bobby McNaught (physio), Gordon Dickson, Bill Gammell, Bob Cunningham, Euan Kennedy, Alan Tomes, Donald Macdonald, Colin Mair, Ron Wilson, Gerry McGuinness. Front row: Ian Barnes, Ian McLauchlan, George Thomson (asst manager), Nairn MacEwan (coach), Tom Pearson (manager), Mike Biggar (captain), Colin Fisher, Jim Renwick, Alastair Cranston, Bill Watson

There was, too, a dangerous lack of experience, particularly in a country where the gulf between club and international rugby was so enormous. Players like myself, John, Colin Deans and Keith Robertson were all just beginning our international careers and there were others who were just as green.

Scotland played some lovely running rugby under MacEwan but all too much of it, I am afraid, was when the game was already lost and won and it did not really count. The trouble, not all of MacEwan's own making by any means, was that we simply could not get enough quality ball. He knew the game and, had he had more experience behind him, I am sure his handling of players would have shown to greater advantage. The tragedy was that he was pitched in without serving his time at lesser representative levels, among which the B Internationals are as valuable to the coach as they are to the players.

Jim Telfer, on the other hand, worked his way up over many seasons and, being the man he is, would be the first to admit that he was at least three times as good a coach by the year of Scotland's Grand Slam as he had been when he took the South Under-21 XV which, incidentally, was the very first occasion when John and I were played as a pair.

In his days as Scotland's captain, with no coach to lighten the load, Jim Telfer had virtually run the show while, of course, he had been for long a focal figure at the Greenyards. Nevertheless, in his early years as a coach, he was mainly concerned about fitness and motivation and, incredible though it is to imagine now, he was actually sacked as the South's coach. Characteristically, he stayed with it and much of the foundation of the 1984 Grand Slam was laid with many of the same players working under him at B International level.

He was a very different coach from the one John and I had first known by the time he took over the Scotland post from Nairn MacEwan. For me, it was my second season in the Scotland team and, in respect of the ball I was getting, the difference between night and day.

Telfer had not wasted his years in waiting. He went to work on the set scrum so that if we did not dominate, we would at least achieve something close to parity, get our share. Knowing that Scotland were so often short of giants, he had given much thought to the lineout and carefully studied how the opposition in the various countries went about it. Realising that he had a great asset in the pin-point throwing-in of Colin Deans, he introduced some imaginative variations and, something I particularly appreciated, got rid of much untidy lineout ball by having first Bill Cuthbertson and then Alister Campbell do the sweeping. Towards the tail, Jim Calder also did some unspectacular but priceless tidying up, his skill at making the ball available proving decidedly useful in this context.

Above all, of course, Telfer worked on the Scotland rucking. He had long ago come to believe that Scotland's way should be the All Blacks' way partly, though not entirely, because the two peoples were not of all that different extraction. As John rightly

Jim Telfer making a point to John Rutherford and Jim Renwick

asserts, behind the scrum the greatest difference Telfer made at once was to the defence, which had been very weak in the immediate past. You do not miss too many tackles when the man calling you to account is Jim Telfer. He had a favourite phrase to the effect that we must leave no stone unturned in our preparation and, as far as was humanly possible, he made sure that we never did. He made use of the study of video, where our own past games were concerned and those of our opponents. He was perhaps inclined to overdo it simply because not everyone could remain so single-minded for so long as he could but there was no question that much of that study did pay off.

His analysis of the enemy was first-class, detailed and accurate, and we always felt we knew all their strengths and weaknesses. He left nothing to chance and, on the morning of an international, would go to the ground to assess the likely

121

conditions, even down to where you could expect a section of the pitch to be sheltered from the wind by the stands.

It is said that Carwyn James, the Welsh coach who guided the 1971 Lions to victory in the Test series with the All Blacks, was a great listener, always willing to hear the opinion of others before making up his own mind. Telfer similarly would let players have their voice and, indeed, having learned from a Scottish rugby writer how the All Blacks at their team talks would call upon certain players to get to their feet and run through their roles in the coming game, he himself made some use of the practice.

After defeat, he would go very quiet and one used to judge it safer to keep out of his way. But, come the next Sunday squad session, just when you were expecting to be torn to bits, he would lift you. It was after some of our greatest victories that he would give us the worst hell, bring us down to earth with a bump. I would endorse John's view that it all made sense psychologically.

At team gatherings, he could be almost unbelievably hard but usually it was on the players whom he admired the most and from whom he expected and needed to get such a lot. On some of the others, who had shortcomings neither he nor they could do anything about, his tongue would be lighter. When we lost, he would invariably shoulder his share of the blame and he learned from his own mistakes, particularly from a tendency, born of sheer zeal, to overwork the squad. He had humour and was very much a players' man in that he saw everything from their angle, but you always knew what you could not say to him. He was one of the team and yet that little bit apart just as I reckon a great coach in rugby, or a great manager in soccer, should always be.

Many in Scotland and beyond asked why, when he was so successful with Scotland, he should have suffered a whitewash by the All Blacks when he was the Lions' coach in New Zealand. I think, and I know John is of the same opinion, that circumstances were so different that the outcome was not really so surprising. When he took over Scotland, many of the players were already his men in that they had grown up in senior rugby under him at various levels in the South, and with the Scotland

Roy Laidlaw, British Lion 1983

B. Scotland had had such a bad spell of results that he was starting from the bottom and so he began by simplifying everything, getting us right back to the basics. What is more, he not only had the players with him but men on the selection committee, such as Ian MacGregor and Robin Charters, who were right behind him.

With the Lions it was just not the same. The Scots in the party used to say that he was not as hard on the Lions as he was on Scotland, but then the Hawick lads used to say that Derrick Grant was never as hard with Scotland as he was with Hawick. I suppose it is natural enough, the difference in being absolutely in your own environment and having to feel your way a little. Besides,the Scotland players knew that Telfer was a selector whereas Lions who fell out with him knew that he would have nothing to do with whether they played for their particular country the following season. That applies, of

Derrick Grant – a tremendous coaching record with Hawick and a fine coach of the South and of Scotland

course, to any Lions' coach and it is something I imagine most of them recognise.

There were all sorts of reasons why the Lions did not do better. The chief one was probably that there were simply not enough great players in the side, nothing like the Lions had had in 1971 with men such as Gareth Edwards and Barry John, Mike Gibson, Gerald Davies and J.P.R. Williams and, of course, Mervyn Davies. 'Merv the Swerve' was really two players in one in that he was a cracking No. 8 and an authentic lineout specialist.

Willie John McBride, the manager, and Ciaran Fitzgerald, the captain, patently had a lot of the necessary credentials but Fitzgerald was in the awkward position that Colin Deans, as the British press and all New Zealand kept reminding him, was playing much the better rugby as his understudy. Where the three of them were concerned, McBride, Telfer and Fitzgerald, the chemistry was clearly not right. Going back once more to the 1971 Lions, long before the Test series was won, it was obvious that they had a great blend in Carwyn James as coach, John Dawes as captain and Doug Smith as manager.

I disagreed with the insistence that there would be no recognisable Wednesday and Saturday sides. That, in theory, might be good for team spirit but it meant that the Test team had scant time to settle. I am told that in 1971 Carwyn James had his sides mapped out for the early matches even before the Lions left Britain though, of course, he had the flexibility to adjustthem as necessary according to form and fitness.

Technically and tactically, nothing handicapped Telfer more than the fact that his forte as a coach was a rucking game and yet fifty per cent of the forwards they gave him were not ruckers but maulers. Indeed, one of the best rucking forwards in Britain, Bill Cuthbertson, was not even summoned when gaps appeared in our ranks through injury. The Lions never got anywhere near the rucking unison which Scotland had achieved by the time of the Grand Slam when Telfer's unceasing demand that, where possible, players stay on their feet really began to bear fruit.

I remember in the Triple Crown match with Ireland, he congratulated me on my two tries. He said, though, that what had gratified him most about the first was not the try itself but that both David Leslie and Colin Deans had managed to remain on their feet and would have turned it into a try if I had been stopped short of the line. He was right, too, because so often when you break, you do not actually score and that kind of support can be the difference between a try or not.

When Jim Blair, the former Scottish footballer who trains the All Blacks as well as many others among New Zealand's sporting élite, visited the Greenyards last winter, he underlined that he was a trainer not a coach. Even so, he still felt qualified to sum up the All Blacks' creed: 'The player with the ball must stay on his feet and there must be a player within a yard of him on either side in support'. Telfer, I wager, nodded in approval.

Colin Telfer, aside from the time and patience he gave towards helping John practise his kicking, deserved his share of the credit in the matter of the Grand Slam for he was Jim Telfer's assistant, his particular responsibility being the backs. John and I both saw him as better suited temperamentally to that subsidiary role than to being the senior man in charge, as he was on either side of the Grand Slam. In 1983 Jim Telfer had temporarily demitted office because of his duties as a Lions' selector while, by 1985, he had stood down as Scotland's coach.

As in the case of Nairn MacEwan, Colin Telfer had been a fine player but had had comparatively little experience as a coach in the sense of working his way up through the different levels. None the less, he was more than a little unlucky both in the loss of key players and in the bounce of the ball.He always gave it his best shot and, as one who captained the side under him, I wished that we had been able to repay him with better results.

Derrick Grant, who had had a tremendous record as Hawick's coach and who had been Colin Telfer's assistant, had a great deal in common with Jim Telfer. Both were Borderers and both had a rugby philosophy which set most store by rucking.

Jim Telfer, in his profession as a schoolteacher, had lived outside theBorders which must surely have been useful to him when it came to dealing with the national team. He had also been much in demand as a captain at assorted strata from club rugby to given matches on Lions' tours. It took Grant a bit of time to be quite as confident and authoritative as Jim Telfer had ultimately become but Grant was good from the first and very good indeed once he was fully into the job. Last season slightly tarnished the record but he and Ian McGeechan had some magnificent results in their seasons together with Scotland.

McGeechan materialised at a time when John was very much at the crossroads, his head buzzing with all the different ideas he had picked up from his opposite numbers in other countries and the national coaches of other lands. McGeechan cleared his mind and proceeded to bring out of him the best rugby of his career, the kind of rugby which had so many acknowledging him as the greatest stand-off in Scotland's history by the time that tragic injury to his left knee brought his playing days to a close.

John and he were soon on precisely the same wavelength, with John persuaded that McGeechan had it in him to transform the back play not only of the national XV but of the game throughout Scotland as the players took his teaching back to the clubs. Just when it was all coming good, McGeechan lost

Ian McGeechan – the best coach of backs since Carwyn James. McGeechan will have charge of Scotland this winter and of the Lions in Australia in the summer of 1989

John and, as he lamented, had almost to start again rather than move forward, building on what had gone before.

McGeechan was adamant that every back should master what he saw as the four basic skills for those outside the scrum – the short pass, the long pass, the loop and the scissors. He was not a great man for set moves but some of those he did design were very perceptive, such as a loop by the stand-off followed by a miss-move. The concept was that the stand-off, by looping, would make it impossible for his direct opponent to drift. He liked his backs to come late on to the pass from depth which made it very difficult for the defence to line up their targets. One drawback, though, was that the Scotland player did not see, until the very last seconds, if at all, the man to whom he was giving the ball. He also wanted his backs to use contact as a form of attack in itself since, if they stood up in the tackle, the support could get in behind the defence. To put it another way, he turned an enemy tackle into an opportunity to forge an opening.

Particularly as Scotland had mobile, ball-playing forwards who could get about the field, he wished the ball played wide when it was possible to do so. The backs themselves had to come round and frequently lend the first support. The choice of such wings as Matt Duncan and Iwan Tukalo probably owed not a little to their strength on their feet and good physique. When the ball was brought inside by a scissors, he looked for a loop to get it back out wide and, of course, he was quick to see how Gavin Hastings increased Scotland's offensive options.

He was an ardent advocate of getting there in numbers not just in attack but also in defence. He sought to have us defend in threes in that one man would be there to make the tackle, another to hit the support and the third to fasten on to any spill of the ball. I remember how chuffed he was when he could point to the video and show that we were getting there not just in threes but in fours.

McGeechan is a quiet man far removed from the public's image of a beer-swilling rugby hearty singing bawdy songs, and there are those in high places who are said to think that he is not hard enough in his dealings with the players. I can only say that neither John nor I can recollect having heard any player say one word against him. A measure of his popularity was that the backs clubbed together to present him with a new dinner jacket because he had always protested, half in jest, that, as a poor schoolmaster, he could not afford to replace the old one he wore which had been heavily overtaken by changing fashion. Some still think that he is more at ease as simply the assistant coach in charge of the backs but the great record he has built up as coach-in-chief with the Scotland B would seem to go quite some way towards refuting that.

John Rutherford

8 The way ahead

In most half-back partnerships, you find one solid player, one attacker; but it is impossible to say whether Laidlaw or Rutherford carries more menace for the defence – ALLAN MASSIE *in A Portrait of Scottish Rugby.*

I think that Roy has an excellent point when he forecasts that, for a country like Scotland who seek to play a game based on athletic, mobile, ball-playing forwards who ruck, the recent laws designed to keep players on their feet will have an increasingly beneficial effect. As he says, older players often find it difficult to change and the laws at times have altered with such bewildering rapidity that you can scarcely blame them for having had their problems.

Of course, it is still perfectly legal for a player to take the tackle on his own terms but the difference nowadays is that the other players have to stay on their feet and cannot dive in on top of him. That can provide wonderfully inviting ball, but much of the ball produced when no-one has gone to ground at all can be equally succulent from the point of view of the backs if it is swift and dynamic and spawned by a pack still driving forward.

One obvious worry for the legislators is the growing fashion for players not yet in contact with the ruck to be taken out beyond the ball. Clearly, no one with a real understanding of what makes rugby the game it is would wish to see it turned into a glorified game of American grid-iron football with obstruction a legitimate art form. Nonetheless, I do think that the interpretation of the referees has to be adult and realistic and based on whether the forwards in question are genuinely driving over the ball to produce quick, clean second phase or are simply wilfully intent on taking players out illegally. It can be a grey area for inevitably it tends to be the best rucking packs, New Zealand's in the Southern hemisphere and, perhaps

*Roy Laidlaw,
captain of
Scotland*

rather more humbly, Scotland's in the Northern who are most often accused of malpractice in this dimension. Not that France, for instance, are always guiltless.

As a back, I sigh for the days when a player who had been tackled had a little bit of time in which to work the ball up to his support as opposed to having to do so immediately, because under the former law that particular kind of continuity was easier to obtain. But I do see how it could also lead to the detested pile-up, and the present law is perhaps no bad compromise.

It always intrigues me to hear that no longer ago than the All Blacks' tour of 1972, which was not all that long before I myself came upon the scene, a great flanker like New Zealand's Ian Kirkpatrick was still singling out the sudden enemy heel against the head as his most nagging worry on the field of play because, as a right-hand flanker, the opposing scrum half could be round the scrum and past him in a twinkling. Heels against the head happen so seldom nowadays that that would surely not apply now if Kirkpatrick were still playing, and I can understand those who lament the passing of what was obviously a good attacking ball. But Roy thinks that if heels against the head were encouraged by, for example, stopping hookers using hand signals to their scrum halves and by strictly compelling the scrum half to stand a proper distance from the mouth of the tunnel, it might lead to a resurgence of collapsed scrums.

Players of past generations argue that there were, if anything, fewer collapsed scrums in the old days because packs were more interested in winning the ball even on the enemy scrum feed than in pressurizing the opposing scrum. I wouldn't know and I doubt if the present legislators would either but there is unquestionably room for some experiment in this area.

All such comparative technicalities pale into insignificance beside the conviction Roy and I share that the differential penalty could be extended, at least for a trial period, to cover all transgressions save foul play and recurring infringement. Recurring infringement, I would agree, is a better phrase than persistent infringement because if you were, say, two points down in injury-time and the other scrum half deliberately got offside twice in succession to stifle your possession then that would be recurring infringement rather than persistent, yet still deserving punishment by a kick at goal.

Roy and I also side with those who, granted such an extension of the differential penalty, would be in favour of all penalties being taken from a spot bang in front of the posts no matter where on the field the offence occurred. After all, if you kick a man on the head it is no less culpable because you happen to be in his twenty-two rather than under your own posts. Nor do we quarrel with the opinion that whereas the dirty player is sometimes seen as a bit of a hero, if he gives away a penalty which necessitates the whole team trooping back to the other end of the pitch for their opponents to exact an almost certain three points by way of retribution, he will be regarded instead as a blankety-blank idiot.

To our mind that would prove a far greater deterrent to foul play than all the other suggestions put forward, including the Welsh sin-bin. With the laws so framed, the present points

Clive Norling – no fewer than six matches without awarding a penalty to either side

values could be left alone, though logic is undeniably with those who reckon it ridiculous that the frequently classic try scored in a corner should offer a much more difficult conversion than a hack-and-chase opportunist try which finishes up under the posts. Apart from that matter of the conversions, and whether they should either be done away with or all kicked from a given spot – possibly half-way between the goalposts and the touchline – the dropped goal is held in some quarters not to be worth three points. As a stand-off, one may be a little biased, but they are not always quite as easy as they look and, what is more, the ball has usually to be won first by the forwards and then distributed appropriately in the face of an enemy doing everything they can to exert a smothering pressure.

Before leaving the laws, one would have to say that Roy and I are no different from innumerable other players in believing that though, as is so often said, it is not the referees who break the laws, they frequently hold the balance between a good and a bad game.

The laws admittedly have grown a great deal more complex with the years but they were never that simple, our attention recently being drawn to the Laws of 1892 when there were already no fewer than forty-two of them together with another twenty-eight paragraphs of Case Law.

One of the most relevant statistics, which is understandably frequently cited, is that when Scotland won the first of their two Grand Slams at the opening of Murrayfield in 1925, the first points recorded at the ground came from a penalty goal by Luddington of England. That penalty goal was, *mirabile dictu*, the first in the Calcutta Cup for thirty years.

It is difficult for a modern player not to conclude that the referees of those days were less obviously in search of penalty offences than their latter-day counterparts, even if it is conceded that the players of bygone eras almost certainly played more readily within both the letter and the spirit of the law than some of their successors.

In this connection, nothing is surely more pertinent than the case history of Clive Norling of Wales. No referee is ever entirely without his critics but few can have been hailed more often as the best referee in the world than Clive Norling, theatrical or not.

When he began, he was often labelled whistle-happy. The match in which Ireland clinched their Triple Crown in 1982 by defeating Scotland at Lansdowne Road was played in a blizzard of penalties, with Scotland missing too many of theirs while Ollie Campbell was adding a dropped goal to the six he slotted in a 21-12 win.

Yet today Norling reckons never to give a penalty in the lineout because, before that brand of infringement can have been committed, the laws relating to the award of a free kick will have been transgressed. On no fewer than six occasions, he has gone through a complete match without giving a penalty to either side and some of those games were keenly contested affairs, not mere friendlies or exhibitions. In fact,he was into injury-time in a tussle between those great rivals, Cardiff and Bath, before, with no-side looming, he at last gave a penalty.

On a slightly different tack, referees from France, South Africa, Australia and New Zealand are frequently accused when they officiate over here of 'contracting out of the laws' and yet so often they have helped to produce a rip-roaring game, thoroughly enjoyed by players and spectators alike. It is difficult not to suspect that there is a moral to be drawn. . . .

Still looking ahead, Scotland will dissipate the advantage given by those intrepid pioneers who braved all the criticism to instigate the national leagues if they continue with the present structure in which Division I, with fourteen clubs, is far too large for the country's resources and in which there is no Scottish Cup as such. It is not too fanciful to suggest that already their new league framework is making a difference to England and, after trailing us so long in that respect, they could suddenly have the advantage in that their leagues are set alongside an established and triumphantly successful national knock-out cup.

A First Division comprising no more than eight clubs playing home and away fixtures would be a vast improvement in Scotland and even eight clubs may really be too many. As for the Scottish Cup, the big guns from the First and Second Divisions would not enter the lists until the later stages.

Neither Roy nor I has the slightest doubt that a Scottish Cup would be good for the game in Scotland in diverse respects and not least in the marketing of the game and in catching the interest of the youngsters, the players of tomorrow. The nearest thing Scotland have had to a Scottish Cup final was the play-off for the Division I title between Hawick and Gala at the Greenyards which drew a five-figure crowd. Again, Roy loved the Cup Final atmosphere of the past season's play-off for the Border League which Jed-Forest won at the expense of Kelso. Roy even put the experience ahead of Jed-Forest's most memorable sevens triumphs.

The introduction of a national cup would require some further restructuring of the season, our view being in any case that the internationals should be a month later in the year in order to give what is the game's shop window a better chance of favourable weather. The Inter-District championship could remain where it is on the calendar because, thanks to the electric blanket at Murrayfield, it does ensure that the country's leading players are guaranteed some games even in the dead of winter.

Any question of reshaping the Scottish season always used to come up against the Borderers' beloved autumn and spring sevens circuits but, though we risk being shot for saying so, neither of us sees the traditional sevens tournaments as remaining sacrosanct indefinitely. The Melrose sevens are a case apart and for myself I have always loved the story of how an S R U secretary once rang the late Bob Brown of Melrose and told him sternly that Melrose had forgotten to apply for permission to stage their sevens and it was now past the stipulated date for doing so. 'Just you drop in on the Greenyards on the second Saturday in April,' advised Bob Brown, cheerfully, 'and you'll soon see whether we are staging our sevens or not!'

However, you just need to look at what has happened to the autumn sevens to realise how times change. The Earlston sevens have moved to a spring date on a Sunday, the Kelso sevens have shifted from a Saturday to the Sabbath and, as for the Selkirk sevens, we received permission to bring them forward to the last Saturday in August.

Old Ned Haig knew what he was doing when he invented

A winning Selkirk seven at their own tournament, but the sevens game no longer commands quite the loyalty which once it did. Back row (left to right): Iain Paxton, Keith Johnston, Nick Bihel, Billy Rutherford. Front row: Colin Anderson, John Rutherford, Brian Walker

sevens, for they have been an invaluable money-spinner for the Border clubs, besides providing some great play and many unforgettable personalities. But many of the clubs in Scotland, who once took them very seriously, no longer do so and even in the Borders some of the greatest sevens enthusiasts fear that the sevens game no longer commands the loyalty that it once did. In days gone by, of course, the Border tournaments did not have to compete with the kind of yardstick now provided by such glamorous events as the Hong Kong Cathay Pacific sevens or this year's Australian Bicentennial International sevens in Sydney.

Jim Blair, the Scot who trains the All Blacks, was shocked by the amount of rugby many of the leading players in Britain play, his opinion being that by playing far too much they not only lost their zest and freshness but had far too little time left for properly programmed training and for practising the individual skills.

In Scotland, the main representative players face the demands of their clubs, their districts and the national squads and, with that in mind, the authorities have to be careful that too much is not asked of amateur players who also have to think in terms of both their jobs and their families.

It often requires commonsense all round and we would freely confess that that is not always forthcoming even from the players themselves, for Roy and I were no better than the next man at turning down yet another often largely meaningless match.

John Rutherford

9 'Left-arm spinner preferred'

Usually, down the seasons, John Rutherford had been so neatly unhurried, letting slip with his kicks and leadership of his scavenging seagulls in the blue shirts. Never rushing, always in control, always perky – no, not perky, that's the word for Welsh fly halfs. Spruce is nearer the mark for Rutherford. He was always beautifully turned out; always upright in both meanings of the word; energy always disciplined and his intellect always twitching, keen to show off the game's classic traditions – FRANK KEATING in the *Guardian,* January 1988.

In truth, Roy Laidlaw swears that he is often more nervous playing for Jed-Forest, where so much can depend on him, than for Scotland, where there is the reassurance of having so many good players about him – NORMAN MAIR in the *Sunday Standard,* January 1983.

That splendid story of how the late Jock Wemyss was not initially given a jersey for the first international he played after the Kaiser's War because, after all, he had played in 1914 and therefore ought still to have one, may be apocryphal for all I know but the fact that so many believed it surely tells a lot about the image the Scottish Rugby Union had for so long. They have come a very long way since those days, especially in the last decade, but there is no denying that the players can still be irritated and upset by how inexplicably pernickety they can be over some things. On the whole, the Scotland players are very well treated and, in respect of their preparation, given every chance. Certainly, the S R U are not miserly when it comes to the considerable expense of fetching players to Murrayfield for extra squad sessions or, if the weather wipes out rugby elsewhere, additional trials-cum-practice games.

Yet if you order an additional sandwich to be brought up to your room or maybe on the night of the match have coffee with

Ian MacGregor – convener of the selectors when Scotland won the Grand Slam and an official who understood the need for better relations between officialdom and the players

your wife in the hotel lounge, you will be billed accordingly. It is an amateur game by definition but, when the players see the crowds they are pulling in, and think of what is going on elsewhere with regard to breaches of the amateur ethic, it's hardly surprising that they find that kind of thing a bit ridiculous.

A cautionary word to the players not to go overboard in the matter of extras would surely be all that was needed to keep the matter within acceptable bounds and if anyone then abused that dispensation, he would have scant sympathy from the rest of the players if the Union made him cough up.

Ian MacGregor, who was convener of the selectors when Scotland won the Grand Slam in 1984, was very much a players' man and one of the best things he did that season was to get some of the senior players together and ask them to tell him their views on such sometimes ticklish matters as tickets, wives, girlfriends and the like.

Nowadays, the S R U pay for the accommodation costs of the wives on the night of the match and, what is more, they have now extended that dispensation to apply similarly to girl-friends. As to tickets, a Scotland player gets two free tickets for the match, the two which any past internationalist is entitled to purchase and the opportunity to buy another six. It sounds generous enough but, though he would never complain, a player like Roy Laidlaw can still be out of pocket simply because he will need to fork out £12 for another ticket if both his small sons as well as his wife want to watch him play.

The players used to writhe at stories alleging that any S R U committee man had access to fifty tickets and some of us thought that rather than allow such rumours to eat into the spirit of the camp, the S R U ought to make public just what the distribution among the various members of the S R U actually was. Many of the S R U work so hard on behalf of the game that no one can grudge them some reasonable perks but the trouble is that when the facts are not available almost any kind of exaggeration is liable to be given credence.

One other aspect of the allocation of tickets surfaced afresh at last season's meeting with the senior players in the Scotland squad. Namely, the conviction held by quite a few of the team that it would not merely be tactful but appropriate if a couple of tickets were sent to a player's employer on the grounds that a modern international player is away so often that such an employer is indirectly sponsoring Scottish rugby.

The relationship between the players and officials is, judging by what past players have told me, probably the best it has ever been in the long story of the international game in Scotland. Yet, as in the matter of the allocation of tickets, players bristle with indignation at unconfirmed tales that whereas in their expenses the mileage allowance is 15p, for the S R U themselves it is 25p. That seems so unjust that I should doubt the validity of the assertion but here, too, since everyone is on the same side, it is surely a foolish thing to keep secret.

Such little niggles apart, the players, make no mistake, greatly appreciate what is done for them. The decision in Mac-Gregor's time to move the players out of the centre of town before an away match, long advocated in at least one corner of the press, has proved an immense success, with Scotland's away record strikingly improved. The St Pierre Golf and Country

Club is perhaps Scotland's favourite away base while, for home internationals, the Braid Hills Hotel on the outskirts of Edinburgh stands very high in the players' affections.

The food, an important element for fit young sportsmen with a big occasion looming, is usually excellent, though the S R U did have to act to make sure that the squad did not make beasts of themselves at the expense of their performance on the field. At one time, the players could eat à la carte on the Thursday evening and at lunch and dinner on the Friday, and you would find some strapping young gluttons treating the menu like the card of a golf course, wending their way steadily through it. Today, the players may dine à la carte on the Thursday evening but thereafter what they eat is more carefully monitored, though the S R U cater to each player's individual preferences.

On tour, it can be still more difficult for the powers-that-be to keep an eye on the players in this sphere. On the Lions' tour of New Zealand in 1983, Jim Telfer, as coach, was forced to ban milk shakes which were being consumed in vast quantities. One afternoon, Jim Calder, Iain Paxton and the Bear – Iain Milne – found themselves in a cafe well off the beaten track and, feeling uncommonly peckish, ordered up hamburgers and milk shakes. Even as their fangs closed on the first bite, the door opened and in came Jim Telfer!

The S R U's medical team have been superb in my time and no one who saw them in action could fail to have been impressed by the part played by the S R U medical officer, Donald MacLeod, and the physiotherapist, David McLean, on Scotland's tour to New Zealand in 1981. Not just Donald MacLeod and David McLean but all the S R U medical staff are more than just part of the official set-up – they are friends, allies and, on occasion, invaluable confidants.

Still within the context of looking after the players, the S R U have come so far from that aforementioned tale of Jock Wemyss that contemporary players can have few complaints concerning the generosity of the kit handed out to them. Generally speaking, it is tasteful, the quality has mostly been good and there has been plenty of it. Sponsorship contracts with the firms concerned may have made it all possible but the S R U still deserve credit for the deals they have struck.

I should hate ever to see the national jersey defiled by commercial advertising or even, though I suppose it could happen, a manufacturer's discreet logo. Otherwise, though, sponsorship seems bound to increase and, since sponsors have to be given value for money, so, too, will the advertising.

I can readily accept that such things as logos and commercial lettering on, for example, tracksuits have to be regulated in terms of size but there are undoubtedly times when such restrictions can seem maddeningly petty – a case in point being the Selkirk tracksuits provided by Border Plant Hire. The lettering was apparently an inch too large and, since we were coming before the television cameras, it had to be covered over with tape.

The commercialisation of the game, and what many see as creeping professionalism, have been burning topics in recent years and never more so than in the World Cup in New Zealand. To be brutally honest, it was not quite true that, as some S R U officials like to have it, the Scotland players were upset at the amount of advertising the All Blacks seemed able to do. Rather what was upsetting them was that All Blacks could apparently do that kind of thing while, back home, a Scotland player was not even allowed to receive a Player of the Year trophy.

The New Zealanders insisted that the Scots had misinterpreted what was going on – contending that, to cite one obvious case, Andy Dalton, in his television commercial for a tractor, was starring as a farmer and not as the All Blacks' captain. At no stage, they pointed out righteously, was the fact that he was an All Black, let alone the captain, mentioned in the commercial. But then, as was remarked at the time, since the All Blacks' captain is as well known in the Land of the Long White Cloud as the Queen is in this country, that was hardly a very convincing defence.

The S R U, so Roy tells me, told the players last year that, in future, they would be permitted to accept Player of the Year awards or, at any rate, the more reputable ones. Yet such things are only on the periphery of the real issue which is what the authorities are going to do about the real anomalies which exist in a game where some unions still endeavour to abide by the

142

John with his wife, Alison, and sons, Grant (six months) and Michael (three)

amateur regulations and others appear to turn a Nelsonic eye to what they know is happening within their borders. In fairness, as with boot money in this country, it is one thing to be aware of it, quite another to obtain the necessary measure of proof.

The various unions are not so naive as many might assume from the fact that they so often do nothing, for they know perfectly well that the players from the Southern hemisphere, who pour into France and Italy, are not all there to study their European cultural heritage or the source of the Holy Roman Empire. Neither, in my experience, the most pressing interests of the typical New Zealand lock forward.

Officials, scarcely less than players, hear all the stories about players in this or that country being given a cafe to run, a flat and a monthly wage, and even within the four Home Unions there was, this season, talk of the players of one famous club being paid from the proceeds of the car park – and, let it be said, it's a mighty big car park.

I do not say for a moment that there are not Scottish players who have transgressed the amateur code or that too many believe that Scotland was exempt from the boot money scandal, but I would say that the game is still more genuinely amateur in Scotland and probably in Ireland than in most of the other major rugby playing countries.

Many would be amazed at just how much out of pocket Roy would be if he were ever to stop and tot up what his rugby career has cost him. Not that he ever grumbles or regrets a moment of it but it does make him laugh when the players and press of other nations assume that rugby must have made him a wealthy man. The day after Scotland beat France in the Grand Slam encounter at Murrayfield in March 1984, the particular here of the hour, Roy Laidlaw, was busy in his capacity as an electrician on the wiring in a public loo in Jedburgh!

Those who played when rugby was truly amateur would frequently take a lot of persuading that they did not have the best of it but whether we like it or not, 'The old order changeth.'

Very few players, if any, and certainly neither Roy nor I, would ever want to see the players paid to play. Nor, indeed, do we think that the game as we know it could stand it.

The biggest clubs in England and Wales might have large enough gates to sustain professional players but it would be impossible for most of the clubs in Scotland and Ireland without indulging in fund-raising activities which would make even staying extant as a club a misery. Kelso are the Scottish champions and when they play Hawick in a crunch championship match, they maybe have a crowd at Poynder Park of some 3,000. That is magnificent when you think of the size of the population of Kelso but how are you going to run a club and pay players when that represents one of the bumper gates of your season?

However, while we never want to see players paid to play, we both believe that the day will come when players will be allowed to cash in on endorsements, advertising contracts, radio and television appearances, books and so forth.

Sundry covert payments are made all over the rugby world

Roy with his wife, Joy, and sons, Scott (seven) and Clark (ten)

already and, since it is happening anyway, surely it would be much better to bring it out into the open and legitimise it.

If some firm or somebody wished to give one or more of Kelso's players money for some endorsement or for opening a shop, that would place no burden on the club and require nothing in the way of a restructuring of the game save for amendments to the present amateur coding.

There would still be those who would breach the spirit if not the letter of that code for, though you could not pay a player, there would be nothing to stop a club offering a player they wanted a few hundred pounds to put his name to the programme notes. There would be other similar dodges but then, long before professionalism cast its shadow over so many realms of sport, which once seemed destined to remain eternally amateur, recruitment of players was apt to prove a decidedly competitive market.

In fact, one of my favourite anecdotes is that of the advertisement in a local paper in a veritable hotbed of village cricket: 'Curate wanted. Left-arm spinner preferred. . .'

John Rutherford

10 A fishy tale and more besides

Laidlaw gave a tremendous performance. He was the only man who was a danger to us – PETER FENTON, coach of Sydney, on Sydney *v.* Scotland 1982.

Rutherford and Laidlaw were the pivot around which the Scottish international game revolved: they were the foundation on which the team was laid – BILL MCMURTRIE in *Rothmans Rugby Year Book 1987*.

Most youngsters have their heroes and at Philiphaugh mine was Mick Linton, the Selkirk and South wing. I was hopelessly prejudiced, of course, but in the eyes of my boyhood he should have had a Scotland cap.

He was a biggish chap of some fifteen stone born inexplicably of tiny parents, his father being the club groundsman around whom stories grew. One year the river burst its banks and so quickly did Philiphaugh flood that he took to the stand as fast as his wee legs would carry him and had to be rescued by boat. The fish farm above Philiphaugh also flooded and suddenly there were trout galore swimming on the pitch. They had been trained to feed off breadcrumbs and so forth and the lads were soon down at the ground and had the trout jumping as they threw them assorted tit-bits.

Mick Linton himself was an abrasively combative wing. There is a story of one young opponent from a rival club taking a terrible buffeting as he closed on Linton who, in full stride and clasping the ball, thrust his head into him as he gave the would-be tackler the roughest of receptions. 'But Mick,' cried his alarmed adversary, soothingly, 'I wasn't really trying to tackle you!'

He saw Bill Gammell, the Edinburgh Wanderers and Scotland wing, as one of those who had usurped his Scotland

Mick Linton, John's boyhood hero, charges down the wing

place and, the next time they clashed following Gammell's cap, Mick made straight for him every time he himself had the ball. When Bill Gammell turned up for the Scotland squad session the next day, the other players thought at first he had been attacked by a giant cat.

Tales about Mick abound; some are either apocryphal or have grown in the telling. But I always liked the story of how, when out shooting, he had inadvertently bagged a swan. Fearful on his behalf of the retribution which might descend upon him, the Selkirk players asked what on earth he had done with it. 'I had it,' said Mick, cheerfully, 'with chips!'

Once Mick Linton, David Bell, my brother James and myself were invited over the border to play for the Public School Wanderers. The hiring of a car to take us there was entrusted to Mick. Scarcely had we reached the M6 than a tyre blew which rapidly led to the painful discovery that there was no jack. James changed the tyre while the three of us, the veins standing out on our foreheads, held the vehicle up manually. In the dark, we were stopped by the police because the lights were not working but they were very understanding and suggested that the trouble could be a loose fitting. They even took surprisingly well the revelation, when they removed the casing, that the real trouble was there was no bulb. Otherwise, as Mick kept pointing out, the car went very well, except that the handbrake on the way home suddenly proved unexpectedly and disconcertingly detachable.

Philiphaugh has its own Kop, a collection of worthies who never miss a Selkirk match home or away. The Rogerson family, the brothers David and George and their two sons – all four of them Selkirk standard-bearers in their time – keep up a ceaseless flow from kick-off to no-side as any Border referee will tell you and yet otherwise you could scarcely meet a more silent quartet. It can be the dickens of a business getting a word out of them.

Another member of the Kop was Cookie Broon who, as a caustic critic, had some memorable lines to his name. He once suggested replacing a Selkirk full back of whom he did not approve with a stick stuck in the ground on the off-chance that it might, from time to time, stop an opponent or the ball, which was something he considered the full back in question never did. He used to be sardonically sceptical concerning team selection and said that each week he would buy the 'wee paper', as we call the local in Selkirk. Once he had made sure that no one had died, he knew the team would be 'same again'.

Yet another habitué is Tucker Scott whose rugby stock in trade is to mark the players out of ten and usually, for he is a man of strong opinions, you are at one extreme or the other. I used to catch his eye across the bar after a match and, when he shook his head, I knew the worst.

Much the same thread of humour runs through all the Border clubs both on and off the pitch and, for all the fierce rivalry of the Border League, they are not averse to demonstrating a united front against the world at large. Sometimes, indeed, you are not too sure whether they are only joking – as, for example, when I was appointed from among six applicants to the physical education staff at George Watson's College. The head of the department, Donald Scott, a Scotland threequarter and a great favourite in his time first at Milntown and then at Myreside, told me that what had swung the balance was that I was the only one who knew where Langholm was!

Even after the players of different clubs have been knocking lumps out of each other in a Border League match, any lingering resentment is usually alleviated by a flash of wit or a jest. Sometimes the thrust will be at the opposition's expense but a player like the inimitable and incorrigible Norman Pender, that massively weighty prop of Hawick and Scotland, rather enjoyed making fun of his own image. Once, after a match with Selkirk, he sat down in the bar and declared, 'That was the dirtiest match I've ever played in. Why, I heard someone kicking me on the head!'

Nearly every referee you meet, even those who are not Borderers themselves, have their own store of anecdotes but one I like as much as any originated before my time and belongs to Scottish rugby's own Burrell Collection. Namely, of the day Jack Taylor, a very fine stand-off for Musselburgh in his playing days and later an international referee, was coming away from Mansfield Park when he was accosted by an old Hawick biddy. 'Jack Taylor,' she enquired, winningly.

Jack, who felt himself that he had had a very good game, admitted modestly that it was indeed he.

'Well, Taylor,' she snarled, her brow darkening, 'when Bob Burrell of Gala dies, you'll be the worst *** referee in Scotland!'

Rich source though the Borderers are of such rugby yarns, they have no monopoly of light-hearted camaraderie. Indeed, one of my fondest memories is of being up in Mull with a close friend from my days at Jordanhill College, my old flatmate, Duncan Swinbanks, and finding that one of the frigates was from Wales and wanted to take on the islanders not at soccer as was normally the case but at rugby.

Mull is so hilly that the only place the match could be played was in the public park with sticks tied to the posts to give them some semblance of the rugby version. The Welsh looked awesomely professional in tracksuits and red jerseys and the officer in charge said grandly that, in order to even up the match, they would play uphill in both halves. In fact, amid great excitement, we beat them and that match sowed the seeds of rugby on Mull.

Another not too dissimilar experience came when I took my wife, Alison, to the Olympics in Los Angeles and, by way of pre-

149

season training, was doing some jogging in the area of Newport Beach to the south of L.A. On a pitch, assorted players were playing touch-rugby and, when I stopped to watch, I was invited to join in, the ring-leader explaining kindly the basic laws of the game and, in particular, that the ball could not be passed forward.

The duffer on such occasions may get a game but that does not mean he will get a pass and I found that I was missed out of everything until at last I got the ball and scored a try. Soon I was having overtures made to me with regard to signing on with the rugby club for the coming season and, thinking the joke on themselves, I am told they dine out on the story to this day.

Rugby, on the social side, is a convivial game and some of the resultant stories are perhaps not fit for family consumption or, as in the case of Roy's false teeth, are borderline. It was after a B international with France at Bayonne that Roy, a great servant of the Scotland B as he was later to be of the full Scotland side, had celebrated not wisely but too well. He was roundly sick down the loo and his false teeth went out, as it were, on the tide. Rather disappointingly, it happened on terra firma rather than, as the story ran at the time, in mid-air for one had always savoured the picture of Roy's false fangs descending from outer space on some puzzled inhabitant of Earth.

Another mishap not unconnected with the quenching of a post-match thirst came at the dinner after the French match at Murrayfield in 1986. One of the new caps, his humour by that time in the evening not noticeably overburdened with subtlety, threw a tomato at a friend and, missing his target, saw it burst on the shirt front of one of the most important representatives of Socttish rugby's chief sponsors. Dod Burrell, alias George Burrell, was then the president of the S R U and, at the next Scotland squad session, he vented his wrath upon the assembled team: 'We're in the midst of negotiations for sponsorship worth hundreds of thousands of pounds and I must say you lot have got us off to a *** fine start!'

Mostly, though, rugby players, no matter how different the backgrounds from which they are plucked, learn fast and the Edinburgh forward who ordered Yorkshire pudding as his

The 'Question of Sport' team. Back row (left to right): John Rutherford, Emlyn Hughes, Nigel Mansell, Bill Beaumont, Linford Christie. Front row: David Coleman and The Princess Royal

sweet did not make the same mistake twice. Of course, the game opens many doors and you meet people whom you would be unlikely to encounter otherwise either socially or in the course of your work or profession.

Royalty attend many games, particularly at international level. In truth, a fortnight after the Scotland team had been presented before the 1983 Calcutta Cup at Twickenham to Princess Anne, Patron of the Socttish Rugby Union and as great a favourite with the players as she is with the sporting fraternity as a whole, they were similarly honoured at Murrayfield in the game with the Barbarians to mark the opening of the new East stand.

'We can't keep meeting like this,' said Roy to the Princess.

'No,' she said, glancing furtively over her shoulder and playing her part beautifully, 'people will talk. . .'

Both Roy and I have been on the B B C's Question of Sport and I had the privilege of being on the programme in which Princess Anne hit Emlyn Hughes, our team captain, with her handbag. She not only entered into the spirit of the occasion but proved every bit as competitive as any of the other panellists – but then, of course, you do not do what she has done in the equestrian world, no matter how good a horsewoman you are, unless you have the necessary fibre and, if she'll pardon the word, guts.

In Scottish rugby in the eighties, many of the officials have been much closer to the players than, by all accounts, was the practice in bygone days and selectors like Robin Charters and Ian MacGregor still know how a player feels. MacGregor was particularly sensitive with regard to making sure that the player who had been dropped did not learn of it first through the media.

The classic instance, which I make no apology for repeating, came in that superbly succinct exchange when he rang Alan Tomes in the dark hours of the night when the Hawick and Scotland lock was already fast asleep. 'Toomba' was none too pleased at having his slumbers thus disturbed. 'Shoot,' he said, tersely.

'You're oot!' said MacGregor.

However, as Roy and I sit, revolving, like Sir Bedivere, many memories, none maybe appeals to us more than that of flying over New Zealand en route to the World Cup to find that we had to circle Auckland because it was too misty to land and eventually to divert to Christchurch where we sat for two hours in the plane on the tarmac. We were in the same pool as the host nation and all touring teams, be it New Zealand to Great Britain and Ireland, the Lions Down Under or what have you, are privately convinced that everything possible is being done to make their task harder.

'Hell,' exclaimed Derrick Grant, with magnificent unreasonableness, 'the bastards are at it already!'

John Rutherford

11 The Bermuda affair

John Rutherford, who yesterday announced his retirement after a career liberally laced with splashes of genius, has enjoyed the affection and admiration of the eighties rugby generation – BILL LOTHIAN *in the Independent,* January 1988.

John Rutherford belonged with the great names. During the 1970s and 1980s Britain has been blessed with some great stand-offs. John Rutherford ranks with Barry John and Phil Bennett as the best of them – STEVE SMITH *in Today,* January 1988.

The Bermuda Triangle is a phrase which will make me wince for the rest of my days and there were times in the weeks before the inaugural World Cup in 1987 when I might not have been too sorry to have disappeared into it myself.

Quite some time before the Calcutta Cup at Twickenham, four members of the Scotland XV, myself, Iain Paxton, Iwan Tukalo and Matt Duncan, had been invited by the Bermudan Rugby Union to take part in their festival in early April.

It was the third time I had been invited and this time I was determined to go. On the first occasion, it coincided with the Barbarians' Easter tour and, since it was the first time I had been asked on that particular venture, it was to Wales I went rather than Bermuda.

The second occasion was at the conclusion of the 1984 Grand Slam and this time the only thing it clashed with was a Scotland squad session. I had been a faithful attender of session after session throughout that season and by then, of course, we knew each other's play inside out. But Scotland were shortly to embark on a ten-day tour of Romania, which was to include a Test match, and Colin Telfer, who had taken over as the chief coach, could not see his way to release me. I was very dis-

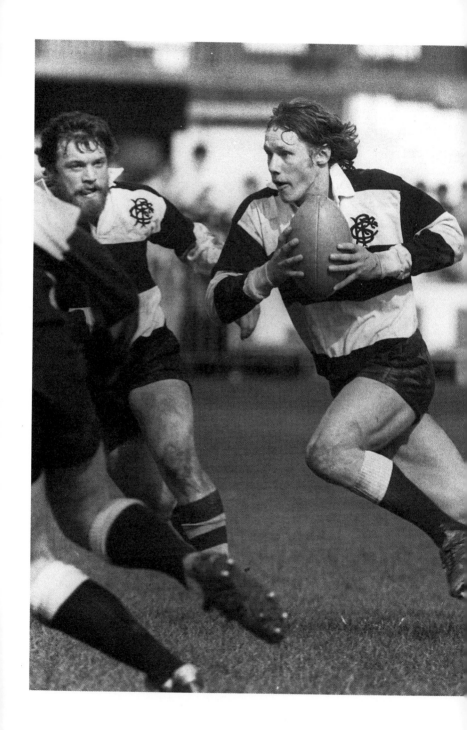

'Rud', as the players call him, on a break for the Barbarians

appointed about it but I suppose, looking back, he felt the session would lose much of its value without the first choice stand-off and possibly feared, too, that allowing me to be away would be seen as weakness on his part in the wake of such a dominant coach as Jim Telfer.

It was not until the day of our departure to Bermuda that we received the letters from the S R U instructing the players in the Scotland World Cup squad not to play any more rugby until the international with Spain at Murrayfield in mid-April. By then it was almost too late to withdraw from the Bermudan trip but, though we had received no formal notification, it would be entirely dishonest not to admit that we had heard the talk and already had a very good idea of the cut-off date.

Not for one moment would I now deny that it was wrong to go. Yet at the time it was not difficult to talk oneself into believing that one was doing nothing particularly heinous. Such trips constitute one of the few perks which come to the amateur rugby player in an age when he has to sacrifice a great deal if he is to make the grade at the higher levels. Even today, when I see quite a few things differently, I marvel at the degree of control Rugby Unions have over amateur players.

A case in point is the attempt by the International Board to impose a time limit within which a player cannot move from his own country to play in another. The players they are after are those they suspect – and suspect is probably too mild a word – of travelling to play in another country for material reward but the ones they will hit, in my opinion, are the young players with no other ambition than to see a bit more of the world while improving their own game by furthering the breadth of their rugby experience.

Where Bermuda was concerned, all four of us genuinely thought that we knew better than the Union and that such a rugby holiday under a warm sun in totally different surroundings was just the thing to recharge the batteries after a long, hard season. Matt Duncan and Iwan Tukalo believed they would best be served by taking it pretty easy but both Iain Paxton and myself thought it would be an ideal opportunity to train really hard in ideal conditions.

The Bermudan Festival is a great rugby weekend and

attracts an appreciative crowd of around 2000 but, though both the Bermudan Irish and the Bermudan XV are laced with invited internationals, the rugby is not too serious nor of a very demanding standard.

I set off down the left wing with Iwan Tukalo, who was playing for the other side, coming across to cover. I made to step inside him off my left foot and something went in my left knee. There had been no physical contact but the pain in my left knee was severe and I was carried from the pitch.

The initial medical examination was compromised by the amount of fluid and bruising, but I knew something was badly wrong. The next day I phoned both the S R U medical officer, Donald MacLeod, and the S R U physiotherapist, David McLean. MacLeod said that he would examine me as soon as I landed in Edinburgh.

At Heathrow, the four of us, who had always been prepared to take what we presumed would be a verbal rap if we were found out but who had obviously hoped that our absence in Bermuda would pass undetected, got a nasty shock. The departure lounge for the Edinburgh shuttle was suddenly filled by young men in blazers.

It was the Spanish team for the international on the Saturday and that meant inevitably that the plane was going to be met by both the media and S R U officials. What is more, I was on crutches which was not going to look too good.

Our tickets were for that particular shuttle and so there was no way we could avoid flying to Edinburgh with the Spaniards. However, once we had landed, we waited at the back of the plane as long as we decently could before disembarking and actually succeeded in avoiding both the media and members of the S R U. My wife, Alison, met me and drove me straight to Bangour Hospital to see Donald MacLeod. There was still too much fluid and bruising for him to give a definite opinion. Though he did not say so, I think he had a very good idea that the damage was quite grave.

I had scarcely arrived home before the telephone rang. It was Bill McMurtrie of the *Glasgow Herald* who had himself received a call from John Mason of the *Daily Telegraph* asking if he could confirm that I had been playing in a match in Bermuda and had been carried off the field injured.

I asked him to hold his hand until I had contacted the S R U myself and then I would get straight back to him. It seemed only minutes after I had telephoned the S R U before both Bill Hogg, the S R U Secretary, and Bob Munro, manager of Scotland's World Cup party, were at my house. They were considerably upset by what I had done, and all the more so in view of the injury. Nevertheless, once they had got that off their chests, I would have to say that they were very fair and helpful.

After they had gone, I phoned Derrick Grant, the Scotland coach, Ian McGeechan, who looked after the backs and who had done so much for me, Jim Telfer and Robin Charters, albeit I missed out on Charters who was on holiday. I certainly did not want any of those men to read it first in the next day's papers, a press release having been hastily drafted.

Even though I grew increasingly optimistic about my chances of making the World Cup, the weeks which followed included the most traumatic days of my life. I knew that I had let down family and friends and, more pertinently, the other players, the coaches and the selectors and what made that feeling all the worse was that the squad had built up such an *esprit de corps* over the years.

I accepted the condemnation in the media which saw the Bermudan jaunt as foolhardy and wrong but I greatly resented some of the over-reaction. Even in the context of the World Cup, which made it a breach of discipline, I could not really see how you could compare an amateur player sneaking off on a rugby trip with the incident in which that wonderful footballer, Jimmy Johnstone, of Celtic and Scotland, floated out to sea in a small rowing boat after a late-night drinking party in what was supposed to be the build-up to an international, or with the unhappy circumstances in which another very gifted Scottish footballer, Willie Johnston, was sent home from a World Cup because drug tests had proved positive.

The criticism which all four of us thought both ignorant and outrageous was contained in the suggestion that we had had our minds more on the forthcoming trip to Bermuda than on beating England in the match at Twickenham which would have given Scotland their second Triple Crown in four seasons.

Even to entertain such a notion is to have no idea of how players think or of rugby at international level. To their credit, one or two of the journalists who took that line have subsequently privately apologised.

Again, I was taken aback, to say the least, by hearing some of the names attached to some of the demands from within the S R U that all four of us be banned from the World Cup. Of course, they were entitled to their opinion, which I do not doubt was founded on good enough motives, but I greatly appreciated the attitude of some of the others which was encapsulated in a typical gesture from the S R U President, Dr Doug Smith.

He had been an outstanding Lions' manager in New Zealand in 1971 and, though you would flout his authority at your peril, he had never lost the ability to identify with players many years his junior who had been brought up in a very different era from his. The four of us had been called to the Braid Hills Hotel to be reprimanded by Bob Munro but we ran into Dr Smith in the hotel foyer: 'Go upstairs and take your medicine,' he said, 'then come downstairs and have a drink.'

The surgeon to whom I had been referred by Donald Mac-Leod, Michael McMaster, a former rugby player himself, reckoned that with time so short before Scotland left for the World Cup he would not go into the knee. Instead, I worked two or three times a day on my hamstrings and quadraceps under the care of Lorraine Sheppard, a physiotherapist who could not have done a better or more conscientious job on my behalf.

My progress was encouraging. Though I did not do a great deal of training with the Scotland squad before we left for New Zealand, I was moving better every day. What I did not do until the eve of the French match was kick with my left foot, which in retrospect was a great mistake. I never took a tackle or did any real physical contact work prior to the French match which marked the opening of Scotland's World Cup campaign.

In fact, I would not have played in that game had not Scott Hastings already been ruled out and I felt that I had to take the chance. I lasted only six minutes. As I instinctively went in to collect a loose ball, I was hit hard in the tackle which I probably rode badly simply because I was apprehensive as to how the knee was going to stand up to the ruder exchanges. I was aware

John's last try for his country, versus England in 1986

at once from the pain, which was very much the same as in Bermuda, that my World Cup was over.

The next day in Christchurch I saw a New Zealand surgeon who is something of a specialist in such knee injuries and he was convinced that the anterior cruciate ligament was ruptured and that I would never play serious rugby again. That was a heart-breaking moment but, on my return home, I decided to give it one more shot. I returned to working under the guidance of Lorraine Sheppard, once again sometimes three times in the one day, and I got back to the point where the following winter I managed two and a half games for Selkirk.

There was, though, no longer any chance of disguising, least of all from myself, that there was something drastically amiss. Michael McMaster sent me to Malcolm MacNicol, a surgeon who had done some great work among the Hibernian and Hearts footballers. He operated on my knee, confirmed that the anterior cruciate ligament was hopelessly ruptured and not only removed it but also took out a piece of lateral cartilage.

I returned to remedial work on the knee with the intention of playing but it became increasingly obvious that there was almost no likelihood of my ever again being in the shape I was before the injury. At 32, I decided against having an artifical ligament replacement, though I may yet do so not because there is the remotest possibility of my playing again but because it may help with my other activities, including coaching.

In the week before Scotland met Ireland at Lansdowne Road in January 1988, I finally made up my mind to retire, the formal announcement being made at the start of the following week.

I am told that the injury could just as easily have happened in training as on that ill-fated Bermudan visit. That thought has in no way lessened the regret I still feel for the embarrass-ment that unhappy episode caused my family and friends, my fellow players and Scotland's coaches and selectors and also, of course, such wonderful and well-intentioned Bermudan hosts as John Kane and Tom Gallagher.

The final irony, bitter-sweet because Roy finished on such a great personal note, was that it was I who had persuaded Roy to have one more season. In the end, he had to go it alone where the two of us had always sworn to go out together.

162

12 From the Scrapbook

International tries

'From a scrum, Rutherford missed out McGeechan. Renwick caught the ball almost on his toes and gave to Hay who handed on perfectly to Irvine, streaming like a tracer-bullet outside him. At precisely the right moment, Irvine stabbed the ball ahead and seemed bound to score only for Slemen, covering across from the other wing, to take the legs from under him in a manner more readily associated with Wembley than Twickenham. Rutherford, running intelligently in support, was up to score but the ludicrous thing is that had Rutherford failed to beat the Englishmen to the touchdown, Scotland would very likely have got a penalty try and an almost certain six points instead of the four they obtained from the unconverted try.'

England *v.* Scotland – Twickenham 1979 (Norman Mair, *The Scotsman*).

'Now Gray took a two-handed catch and brought the ball down, the Scottish forwards driving at the front before turning the ball back to Laidlaw whose pass missed Rutherford and was collected by Renwick. The Hawick centre punted on high and diagonally. With the French defence in a terrible tangle after Bustaffa had spilled the catch, Rives killed the ball, albeit not illegally. For a moment it seemed that the ball was not going to come back, that the referee, John West, must blow for a scrum – but he waited and Scotland heeled for Laidlaw to serve Rutherford who sliced through the torn defence on the yawning blind side.'

Scotland *v.* France – Murrayfield 1980 (Norman Mair, *The Scotsman*).

John scoring against France at Murrayfield, 1980

'As England turned the Scotland scrum close to the visitors' line, Gray picked up and rose from the nether regions to toss the ball back to Rutherford who gathered and carved clean through the England defence to score at the posts. Irvine kicked the goal.

Scotland *v.* England – Murrayfield 1980 (Norman Mair, *The Scotsman*).

'As Scotland attacked and swept first left and then right, Munro was finally pulled down with Irvine up among the thirsting Scots. Caussade's hasty clearance was charged down and Colin Deans adroitly flipped the ball away to Rutherford. The stand-off was conscious of seemingly half the population of France to his left and, as he accordingly slipped blind, of

164

Codorniou, or so he thought, going across him to leave him to the cover. In a flash he was through and clear and running round to ease the conversion, the kind of try he makes look deceptively simple.'

France *v.* Scotland – Parc des Princes 1981 (Norman Mair, *The Scotsman*).

'But then from nowhere appeared Roy Laidlaw breaking clean through the Irish lineout and putting Rutherford in the clear to score his fifth try for Scotland. Irvine converted and the Scots were ahead.'

Ireland *v.* Scotland – Lansdowne Road 1982 (Chris Rea, *The Scotsman*).

Another Rutherford try, versus France at Parc des Princes, 1981

'Rutherford's try, his sixth for Scotland and the third in his last three matches against France, was the result of the determined efforts of the forwards, whose rucking was such a vital factor in this win. It originated at the lineout where, though the Scots finished well in arrears, they did win some important possession. White deflected and Baird, mercifully released from his term of solitary and looking every inch the genuine article, came in from the left wing to take Johnston's pass. Baird linked with White and the ball fell for Laidlaw. The scrum half fed Cuthbertson who led the first charge, Deans was at the forefront of the second and when finally Rutherford took Laidlaw's blind-side pass, he found little in the way of French resistance.'

Scotland *v.* France – Murrayfield 1982 (Chris Rea, *The Scotsman*).

'In view of the capriciousness of the wind, Wilson might have stood closer to Laidlaw, some of whose passes fell short of the mark. The scrum half, perhaps as a result of the additional responsibilities of captaincy or perhaps because of Wilson's limitations, took a little too much on himself but never has a more wholehearted player donned the Scottish jersey and his try, his first for Scotland, was beautifully taken. From a scrummage, he shot off on an ever-widening arc outside McGrath and Slattery. Dod's conversion attempt from close to touch rebounded off the posts and, in the end, those two points were all that separated the sides.'

Scotland *v* Ireland – Murrayfield 1983 (Chris Rea, *The Scotsman*).

'With their scrummage under considerable pressure, the Scots wisely decided not to delay in the set-piece. The ball rocketed through channel one. Laidlaw scurried back to retrieve and, taking advantage of England's eight-man shove, he went round Jeavons, stepped inside Davies and drove through Hare and Scott for the try which Dods, who turned in another solid display at full back, converted.'

England *v.* Scotland – Twickenham 1983 (Chris Rea, *The Scotsman*).

Roy scoring an unforgettable try against England at Twickenham in 1983

'As they had done in the first half, the Lions began the second period in brilliant fashion. In midfield, Iain Paxton hacked the ball on to the right, to stretch the defence. The Lions won the ruck brilliantly, the backs spun the ball across the line to Roger Baird on the left wing, who ran wide to try to round Wilson. As Wilson tackled him into touch, Baird threw the ball inside; Gwyn Evans's pick-up off his toes was magnificent and he got his pass away to John Rutherford, whose burst just took him over the line as he was tackled. "The try of the series", was how the All Blacks' coach, Bryce Rope, described it afterwards.'

All Blacks *v.* British Lions – Third Test at Carisbrook, Dunedin 1983 (Karl Johnston, *The Lions in Winter*).

'The lion-hearted Roy Laidlaw, whose rehabilitation from the pounding he took in New Zealand has been a slow but steady process, burst forth with two marvellous tries scored as only he knows how. One from a ruck, the other from the base of a scrum. His absence from the after-match function was the one dampener on the celebrations, because he more than anyone else had epitomised the spirit and determination in the Scottish side this season. For the first of those two tries, which set Scotland on their way to their first Triple Crown since 1938, Paxton won a lineout in the Irish twenty-two and Alister Campbell peeled. From the ruck, Laidlaw scurried blind, checked, came inside and dived over. The second was almost a carbon copy of the try he scored against Ireland last year as he exploited flaws in Ireland's defensive organisation at the set-piece, running blind from a scrummage. In scoring that second try, he evaded the tackles of both Duggan and Crossan.'

Ireland *v.* Scotland – Lansdown Road 1984 (Chris Rea, *The Scotsman*).

'On the journey over, the conversation touched on the fact that Ireland would be so busy looking for Laidlaw swinging to starboard that they might well prove vulnerable were he to go down the port side. It worked exactly as Scotland had planned. John Beattie picked up at the base of the scrum to release Laidlaw breaking left, the scrum half selling Dave Morrow a dummy worthy of the legendary Ross Logan before darting away to score what was his fifth try for Scotland.'

Ireland *v.* Scotland – Lansdowne Road 1986 (Norman Mair, *The Scotsman*).

'A pass hurled from Colclough to Andrew's ankles defeated the stand-off. Finlay Calder who, in his support play, would have earned many an approving nod from Graham Mourie himself, plucked the ball off the floor brilliantly and gave it to John Beattie. His lob pass was accepted by Laidlaw who passed to Rutherford. With a devastating sidestep off his left foot, Rutherford beat the covering Mike Harrison on the inside, three other Englishmen being simultaneously jerked on to the wrong foot like puppets on the same string. The stand-off's turn of foot took him to the line for the try with which he equalled Herbert Waddell's remarkable bag of seven tries in only fifteen internationals.'

Scotland *v* England – Murrayfield 1986 (Norman Mair, *The Scotsman*).

Roy crosses the Irish line at Murrayfield in 1987 and cleverly keeps the ball off the ground preparatory to running round behind the posts

'Scott Hastings and Gavin Hastings linked to set up a ruck from which Rutherford broke blind before lobbing a nicely judged pass inside to Tukalo. Milne was in support and, as he was brought down, made the ball available for Laidlaw. The scrum half shaped as if to pass out before, in almost one and the same movement, wheeling to slip through over the Irish line, keeping the ball off the deck as he came down on an elbow before running round to dot down behind the posts. Alas, the referee, England's Roger Quittenton, had not seen Laidlaw cleverly protecting the ball from touching the turf in order to leave Gavin Hastings with a conversion from in front of the posts and gave the try where he had first come down. The kick failed.'

Scotland *v.* Ireland – Murrayfield 1987 (Norman Mair, *The Scotsman*).

Laidlaw's Corner at Lansdowne Road, 1988, and Roy's sixth try against Ireland

'In the shadow of half-time, the try came. As the ball broke out of the side of the Irish scrummage on their own line, Laidlaw pounced and threw himself over for what was his sixth try against Ireland in full internationals and his sixth in six matches at Lansdowne Road, one of those games being a B international. Moreover, it was in that corner of a foreign field known since 1984 as Laidlaw's Corner.'

Ireland *v.* Scotland – Lansdowne Road 1988 (Norman Mair, *The Scotsman*).

John Rutherford's dropped goal record

Scotland *v.* Australia 1981	1 dropped goal
Scotland *v.* Ireland 1981	1 dropped goal
Scotland *v.* England 1982	1 dropped goal
Wales *v.* Scotland 1982	1 dropped goal
Australia *v.* Scotland 1982	1 dropped goal
Scotland *v.* All Blacks 1983	2 dropped goals
Scotland *v.* Wales 1985	2 dropped goals
Scotland *v.* Ireland 1987	2 dropped goals
Scotland *v.* Wales 1987	1 dropped goal
TOTAL	12 dropped goals

Record of 35 internationals

Scotland v. England

		For	Against
1980	(H)	18	30
1981	(A)	17	23
1982	(H)	9	9
1983	(A)	22	12
1984	(H)	18	6
1986	(H)	33	6
1987	(A)	12	21

3 WINS, 3 DEFEATS, I DRAW

Scotland v. France

		For	Against
1980	(H)	22	14
1981	(A)	9	16
1982	(H)	16	7
1984	(A)	21	12
1985	(A)	3	11
1986	(H)	18	17
1987	(A)	22	28
1987	(A)	20	20

4 WINS, 3 DEFEATS, I DRAW

Scotland v. Wales

		For	Against
1981	(H)	15	6
1982	(A)	34	18
1984	(A)	15	9
1986	(A)	15	22
1987	(H)	21	15

4 WINS, I DEFEAT

Scotland v. New Zealand

		For	Against
1981	(A)	4	11
1981	(A)	15	40
1983	(H)	25	25

O WINS, 2 DEFEATS, I DRAW

Scotland v. Australia

		For	Against
1981	(H)	24	15
1982	(A)	12	7
1982	(A)	9	33

2 WINS, I DEFEAT

Scotland v. Ireland

		For	Against
1980	(A)	15	22
1981	(H)	10	9
1982	(A)	12	21
1984	(A)	32	9
1985	(H)	15	18
1986	(A)	10	9
1987	(H)	16	12

4 WINS, 3 DEFEATS

Scotland v. Romania

		For	Against
1984	(A)	22	28
1986	(A)	33	18

I WIN, I DEFEAT

John's history

4.10.55 Born in Selkirk to William and Helen Rutherford
1960   Philiphaugh Primary School
1967   Selkirk High School
1970   South Schools Under 15 *v.* Welsh Schools, Galashiels
1971   Welsh Schools *v.* South Schools, Swansea
1972   Head Boy Selkirk High School
        Captain South Schools in Triple Crown *v.* Edinburgh, Glasgow, North and Midlands
        Captain of Selkirk YC in winning semi-junior championship
        Scottish Schools *v.* English Schools, Galashiels
        First game for Selkirk at Gala Sevens – 4 seasons as Captain
1974   Jordanhill College (Scottish School of Physical Education)
        Scottish Colleges *v.* English and Welsh
1977   Qualified as teacher (Dip Phys Ed)
        Scottish tour to Far East
        Teaching post George Watson's College
1978   Scottish B *v.* Ireland B
        France B *v.* Scotland B
        Married Alison
1979   First game for Scotland *v.* Wales
        Selkirk tour to Canada
1980   Scotland tour to France
        Adidas Gold Boot award
1981   Scottish tour to New Zealand
        Man of the Match in Second Test *v.* All Blacks
        Position with Bristol and West Building Society
1982   Hong Kong Sevens (first of 4 times)
        Scotland tour to Australia
1983   British Lions tour to New Zealand
1984   Grand Slam
1985   First son born (19.4.85) Michael John
        Position with Scottish Mutual Assurance Society

1986 Rugby World Player of the Year
   Rothmans Player of the Year
   Joint Five Nations Champions with France
1987 World Cup in New Zealand
   Second son born (10.11.87) Grant William
1988 Retired from rugby

   Played 42 times for Scotland
   Scored 7 tries and 12 drop goals
   Also represented Barbarians and French Barbarians

Roy's history

5.10.53 Born to Jemima and Ian Laidlaw
1958 Parkside Primary, Jedburgh
1965 Jedburgh Grammar School
1968 House Captain and Rugby Captain
1968 First game for Jed Thistle R.F.C.
1969 Apprentice Electrician
1969 Won Border Semi-Junior League
-70 Played 4 games for South Semi-Juniors
1971 First game for Jed-Forest R.F.C. – 5 seasons as Captain
   South Under-21 – 4 games 2 as Captain
1973 First game for South v. Argentine
   Record 68 games – 18 tries
   Captained South to wins over Wellington, Fiji + 1
   Grand Slam District Championship
1974 Scottish Select v. Dutch National XV
   Won Melrose Sevens
1975 First game Scotland B against France at Melrose
   Record 7 games – 6 Tries
   Scottish seven for Irish Centenary sevens
   Won Jed sevens
   Married Joy

1977	First son born – Clark Roy
	Toured Far East
1978	First time as Scotland Replacement
1980	First game for Scotland against Ireland
	Scottish tour of France as Captain
	Second son born – Scott David
1981	Scottish tour – New Zealand
1982	Scottish tour Australia
1983	First game as Scottish Captain against Ireland
	British Lions tour of New Zealand – 4 Tests, 14 Games (2 as Captain)
1984	Scotland Grand Slam
	Scotland tour of Romania
1986	Joint Five Nations Champions with France
1987	World Cup
1988	Retired from rugby

Played 47 games for Scotland
Scored 7 Tries
5 games as Captain
Also represented Barbarians